THE HISTORY OF
PUNISHMENT

THE HISTORY OF
PUNISHMENT

LEWIS LYONS

amber
BOOKS

First published in 2003 by
Amber Books Ltd
Bradley's Close
74–77 White Lion Street
London N1 9PF
www.amberbooks.co.uk

ISBN 0-9544356-2-1

Project Editor: Michael Spilling
Design: Hawes Design

British Library Cataloguing in Publication Data: A catalogue record for this book is available from the British Library.

Printed and bound in Italy by: Eurolitho S.p.A., Cesano Boscone (MI)

CONTENTS

INTRODUCTION
Law and Justice 6

CHAPTER ONE
Early History 10

CHAPTER TWO
From Moses to Mohammed 28

CHAPTER THREE
Democracy & Law: the European Legacy 52

CHAPTER FOUR
India and China 70

CHAPTER FIVE
Corporal Punishment 84

CHAPTER SIX
Throwing Away the Key: Imprisonment 102

CHAPTER SEVEN
Torture 126

CHAPTER EIGHT
The Death Penalty 154

CONCLUSION
Punishment Today 182

Bibliography 188

Index 189

INTRODUCTION

LAW AND JUSTICE

I n the Palaeolithic caves of Addaura in Sicily, there is an engraved scene of several standing human figures grouped around a crouching man, who appears to be tied up so that he would strangle himself if he tried to stand. Thought to be the earliest record of punishment, this evidence seems to show that punishment has existed for as long as human society. Punishment, for the purposes of this book, is defined as a penalty imposed by the state on an offender who has committed a crime. Crimes are whatever actions the state defines as crimes. In prehistoric societies, offenders were judged and punished by the group and crimes were actions deemed to be a danger to the community. As settlements grew, the need arose for permanent social structures and individual or clan vengeance was replaced by state punishment. Crimes were still defined as actions that threatened the stability of the community, but were also more closely identified with actions that threatened the economic and political power of the ruling élite.

Crimes have differed as widely as the societies that defined them. Citizens of Sparta could be whipped for being too fat. In Rome, men and women who had not married by the ages of 25 or 20 respectively were fined. In England it has been a capital offence to rob a rabbit warren, cut down a tree, marry a Jew or deface Westminster Bridge. In Singapore, the importation or distribution of chewing gum is punished by a fine of up to $10,000 or 12 months' imprisonment. In each of these cases, each society had its reasons for defining these acts as crimes. In Singapore, chewing gum was banned because vandals used it to wedge Metro train doors shut. In a small, prosperous, highly ordered society that already had extremely stringent litter laws, the chewing gum ban does not seem so out of place. The Roman law requiring marriage was brought in at a time of falling population, when the authorities decided they needed more children for the future fields and armies of the Empire. The death penalty for defacing Westminster Bridge is perhaps harder to explain although it makes slightly more sense in context. It was one of hundreds of other capital crimes that were part of a 'get tough' package of legislation.

LEFT: Justice, with scales in her left hand, representing judgement, and a sword in her right hand, representing punishment. Throughout history, societies have considered the question of the appropriate punishment for crimes.

CHANGING IDEAS OF PUNISHMENT

The book is divided into two parts. The first four chapters are a historical overview of the main currents of penal thought and practice as established by the first civilizations in Europe, the Middle East and Asia, all of which form the basis of law and punishment in modern times. The last four chapters are a survey of the four main methods of punishment: imprisonment, corporal punishment, the death penalty and a consideration of torture, once a part of the judicial process and still practised clandestinely throughout the world. It is not a comprehensive history, something impossible in a work of this size, but an examination of the key events and currents of thought.

For there to be state punishment, there must first be a state. The state developed as humans made the transition from nomadic hunter-gatherer societies with little need for permanent hierarchy to the complex, highly stratified societies of the first cities. The development of writing made it possible to record commercial transactions, contracts and, eventually, legal codes. The earliest complete legal code in our possession is the Babylonian Code of Hammurabi, famous for its reliance on sympathetic punishment, 'an eye for an eye'. The Code of Hammurabi was a blueprint for later legal codes, the Biblical laws of the Hebrews and the Islamic laws of Sharia, the laws of ancient Greece and Rome, and the legal codes of Europe.

Other legal systems developed outside the Mesopotamian tradition. The Indian Laws of Manu and the Chinese Tang Code reflect very different social, moral and religious practices, yet clearly perform the same functions as other legal codes. The primary function is that of legitimizing the social power of the ruling élite. In the Laws of Manu, religion is used to justify state punishment and to claim moral authority for the position of the ruling Brahman caste. The Tang Code is one of the best examples of a legal code serving as an extension of state power, enabling punishments to be uniformly applied throughout a huge and diverse empire.

The main methods of punishment – imprisonment, corporal punishment and death – have not changed since ancient times, although the practices and the legal justifications may differ from one society to the next. The only real development in penal practice took place in the 18th century, when judicial torture was ended in Europe and imprisonment gradually became the main or only method of punishing serious offences.

Corporal punishment and the death penalty also fell out of use and in many cases were abolished. The rise of prisons corresponded with a new emphasis, to at least some degree, on the reform of the offender. Although the drawbacks of imprisonment were soon apparent, it has been impossible to find an alternative.

'FOR ZEUS ORDAINED THAT FISHES AND WILD BEASTS SHOULD EAT EACH OTHER, FOR THEY HAVE NO JUSTICE; BUT TO HUMAN BEINGS HE HAS GIVEN JUSTICE, WHICH IS FAR THE BEST.' (HESIOD, WORKS AND DAYS)

WHY PUNISH?

Today, as in Hammurabi's time, retribution, incapacitation, deterrence and reform remain the aims of punishment. At different times and places, one of these aims has dominated, but penal regimes contain differing proportions of all four. The 20th century saw punishment develop in two distinct directions. In the second half of the century, Europe led the way in abolishing the death penalty and in placing increasing reliance on non-custodial sentences, crime prevention, rehabilitation and treatment. At the same time, other countries moved towards ever-harsher penal regimes. The death penalty fell out of use and was briefly abolished in the United States, but is now enforced with renewed vigour. A strict definition of Sharia is now being applied in countries that had intermittently or never before applied it. The usual justification for strict penal regimes is deterrence, although the evidence shows, more often than not, that stricter penalties do not reduce crime. In ancient Athens, Draco imposed the death penalty for virtually every crime. Rather than deterring crime, Draco's harsh legal code provoked civil unrest and eventually had to be repealed. The true motives for imposing stricter penal regimes are political; executions may or may not deter potential criminals, but they do demonstrate that the government is 'tough on crime'.

ABOVE: 'Elgarine is drawn to pieces' for the crime of treason, at the command of Indulph, prince of Cumberland, in this 16th century illustration. Damiens, the would-be assassin of France's King Louis XV, suffered a similar fate in 1757.

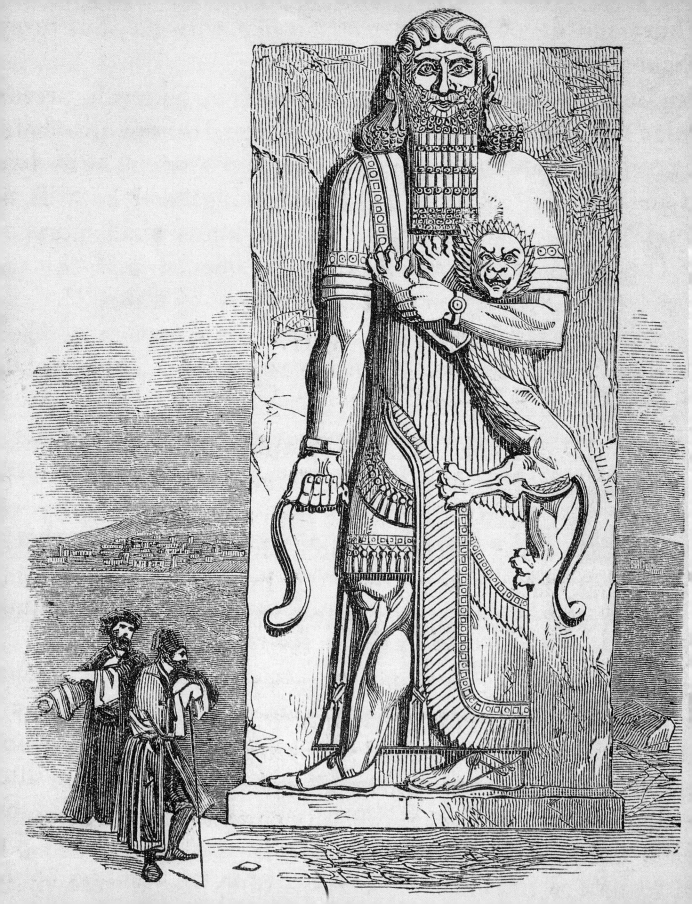

CHAPTER ONE

EARLY HISTORY

There has been punishment for as long as there has been human life. In early tribal groups, the community took responsibility for punishing whatever it considered a crime. As humans developed agriculture and settled in villages, towns and, eventually, cities, religious and secular élites developed, promoting moral and social codes of behaviour and punishing transgressors.

The first true humans, *Homo erectus*, emerged in the East Indies and Africa some one and a half million years ago. From this time until the emergence of the first civilizations that left us written records a mere 5000 years ago, we can only make assumptions about the nature of prehistoric societies and their concepts and methods of punishment. These assumptions are based on archaeological evidence, comparison with the earliest literate societies, and our knowledge of modern nomadic and hunter-gatherer groups.

Until about 10,000 years ago, humans lived as foragers in small multi-family groups that were loosely linked to a community of a few hundred to a few thousand individuals. Before the emergence of large and complex human societies, there would probably have been no kings or rigid social hierarchy. Behavioural codes and moral values were passed on from generation to generation, based on what was best for the group or tribe as a whole.

As hunter-gathering gave way to farming, settlements developed and grew. Çatal Hüyük in modern-day Turkey, settled in about 7400 BCE, had as many as 6,000 inhabitants. In these more complex societies the need arose for political and legal structures and the state began to take over the role of punishment, or at least of judgement, that was formerly assumed by the family or community. The first attempt to control private vengeance was the *talio* (Latin for 'retaliation'), designed to prevent the escalation of blood feuds by deciding that one retaliatory act – perhaps the death or mutilation of the offender – would be enough to pay the debt to the victim's family. The state in effect dispensed punishment on behalf of the offended family; there was no concept of criminal law prosecuted directly by the state.

LEFT: Gilgamesh, the Sumerian King of Uruk, reigned around 2700 BCE and was the subject of many legends, compiled in the world's first epic poem, the *Epic of Gilgamesh*, written in about 2000 BCE.

BELIEF SYSTEMS

It seems likely, by comparison with modern tribal societies such as those of central Australia, that early human social groups were egalitarian, simply since sharing food and resources was the best way to ensure the group's survival. Egalitarian behaviour set early humans apart from social groups of apes, where individuals compete for status and a dominant male monopolizes a disproportionate amount of sex, food and other resources. In early human societies, any attempt to monopolize resources or set oneself above the others would have jeopardized the group's survival and so was probably one of the first 'crimes' to be identified and punished.

It also seems likely that one of the first crimes was incest. Kinship was the strongest binding force in prehistoric societies, and the presence of the incest taboo in virtually every society on earth suggests an origin in prehistory. There were also likely to have been religious offences, such as touching or defiling a sacred object. The evidence here is by analogy with tribal societies in North America, Africa, Polynesia and elsewhere, who prohibit and punish the touching and defiling of sacred objects such as totem poles. Sacred objects – or at least, objects that can only be interpreted as having had a religious or ritual function – have been found at most late prehistoric sites.

Violence was a way of life in prehistory, carried out routinely in defence of the group. Certainly, among nomadic hunter-gatherer groups, violence is unlikely to have been a punishable offence in itself. Violence by other members of the tribe against family and clan members was another matter and was punished severely, most probably by retaliatory violence – the first 'blood feuds.'

Clan loyalty, however, lived on into the historical age. Most early legal systems favoured the ruling families or castes; for the same offence, nobles would be punished by fines or banishment, while commoners faced corporal punishment or execution. The state's justice was often no less violent than the old blood feuds had been.

RIGHT: The life of Kalahari tribespeople has strong ethical dimensions, yet the simplicity of their circumstances has made it unnecessary for codes of law.

CIVILIZATION

It was not until about 5000 BCE that a culture created the social organization that would allow it to grow in size and complexity and to eventually produce the first cities and the first civilization: the Sumerians of Mesopotamia. Encompassing the territory of modern-day Iraq, Mesopotamia means 'between the rivers' and refers to the land between the Tigris and Euphrates rivers. Over more than 5000 years, a succession of diverse peoples migrated to and settled throughout the region, developing rival cities and city-states who vied for power in a succession of wars and shifting alliances.

Mesopotamian civilizations were the first to study the stars, use wheeled vehicles, build arches and write epic poems. They invented the sexagesimal system of mathematics, which established the rule of 60 minutes in an hour and 12 inches in a foot. Sumer, the region of southern Mesopotamia where the rivers meet, saw the development of cities, social and political institutions, bureaucracies, a money economy and writing. During the Sumerian Uruk era (3900–3100 BCE), Uruk (modern Warka) was the largest and most impressive city on earth for 400 years, with a population at the end of the era of 10,000 to 50,000 or more. It was surrounded by a high city wall and was full of magnificent ziggurats – temples set on huge stepped pyramidal bases. Such was its importance that Uruk (referred to as 'Erech') and its ruler Nimrod, the legendary founder of the Babylonian Empire, were mentioned in The Bible:

> [Nimrod] began to be a mighty one in the earth … and the beginning of his kingdom was Babel, and Erech, and Accad …
>
> (*The Bible*, Genesis 10:10)

City life in Uruk revolved around the temple, through which a complex social hierarchy and real political and economic power first developed. It is thought that the high priest was the unrivalled spiritual and political leader of Uruk. In the absence of much private entrepreneurship, the temple was responsible for most of the city's economic activity. It employed a huge number of skilled artists and craftspeople and maintained and educated a 'knowledge class' of architects, planners, administrators and, eventually, scribes. Temple compounds had large complexes of storage rooms for agricultural produce for feeding hundreds of craft specialists and labourers. Its role in the storage, distribution and exchange of goods and its large administration and workforce led directly to the development of writing. From about 3400 BCE, an early form of cuneiform writing was in use. It developed out of the need to keep records and contracts for the goods.

Later, as trade flourished, examples of writing were also found in private houses, which were initially related to economic activity. Although it remained an elite practice, writing gradually spread to uses such as diplomacy between kings, the recording of songs, political propaganda, letters, poetry, such as the Gilgamesh epic, and, most importantly, the drawing up of legal codes. As one city-state conquered another on the plains of Mesopotamia, each regime proclaimed a new set of laws and principles. A legal code is a society's defining document, a statement of principle and a warning to those who oppose its authority. Among the earliest surviving written records, these legal codes help us to piece together a much clearer picture of law and punishment in early history.

THE DEVELOPMENT OF WRITING: THE TOKEN THEORY

Why did writing develop in Mesopotamia when it did? Archaeologist Denise Schmandt-Besserat's 'token theory' is accepted by scholars as the most likely scenario.

Clay tokens averaging 2cm (¾in) in length and in a range of approximately 20 shapes (cones, discs, spheres and partial spheres were most common) had existed since Neolithic times when they were used for keeping records of crops. In the Uruk period, many new complex shapes were added, reflecting the increased number of commodities being traded. Tokens also began to be used to record contracts. In the case of a contract for shipment of goods, tokens were encased in a clay 'envelope' called a *bulla*, and one or two different seal impressions were made on the clay to confirm its contents. On arrival, the shipment was verified against the contents listed in the *bulla*.

To avoid destroying the *bullae* to check the contents, traders began marking the contents on the outside of it by pressing the tokens into the clay. With the parties' seals and the contents of the *bulla* displayed on the outside of the envelope, the tokens inside were now redundant. Traders began to rely on symbols to record their transactions and as these symbols became more complex, writing emerged.

Early legal codes

The earliest legal code discovered is that of Ur-Nammu, founder of the Third Dynasty of Ur in about 2050 BCE. However, there is evidence to suggest that written laws existed before this date. A reference to written law was made in about 2400 BCE, when Ur-Engur, king of Ur, stated that he administered justice 'following the laws of the gods.' Later, Urgakina, king of Lagash, made another reference to written laws when he claimed to have compiled all existing statutes into one code in about 2350 BCE. Although his written code has not been found, a reform document that makes reference to it has been discovered. In it, Urgakina claims that his legal code declares that the entire population has the right to know the justification for each conviction and punishment. He also claimed that his legal reforms were made to end the people's oppression and abuse by the nobles, and also refers to a power struggle between temple and state.

It is likely that Urgakina's legal code was a blueprint for later Mesopotamian codes. All of them are based on similar legal principles and even have the same structure: a prologue proclaiming the king's divine appointment to rule the city, the main body of statutes, and, finally, a warning that those who do not follow the king's laws will be cursed.

BELOW: Gilgamesh, assisted by Enkidu, slays the 'Bull of Heaven' sent by the goddess Ishtar to wreak vengeance on Gilgamesh and his city after he spurned her sexual advances.

Urgakina's reform document gives few examples of punishments, but the document does state that robbers and adulterous women were stoned to death with stones inscribed with their crimes. It's thought that the reasoning behind the harsh penalty for female adultery was that this act could weaken the family bloodlines. It is likely that the Sumerians practiced some form of ancestor worship, so harming the bloodlines would have been seen as sacrilege. In any case, adulterous women continued to receive the death penalty in the Code of Hammurabi, in the ancient Hebrew laws and even in classical Greece.

Ur-Nammu's Code

The poorly preserved tablet containing Ur-Nammu's Code is not the original but a copy made several centuries later. The prologue proclaims Ur-Nammu's selection by the gods as ruler of Ur and lists his achievements, including the elimination of official corruption, the institution of a uniform system of weights and measures, and the introduction of social and moral reforms. The prologue then states that the purpose of the code was to ensure that: 'the orphan should not become the prey of the rich, the widow the prey of the powerful, and the man of the shekel the prey of the man of the mina.' (A mina was a unit of currency worth sixty shekels.)

The tablet is so badly damaged that only five laws can be made out and even these are not very illuminating. One of the statutes refers to a trial by water ordeal, while another concerns returning a slave to his rightful owner. These are the other three:

> If [a man to a man with an instrument] … has cut his foot, he will have to pay ten silver shekels.
>
> If a man to a man with a weapon the bones of … has broken, he will have to pay one silver mina.
>
> If a man to a man with an instrument has cut the nose, he will have to pay two-thirds of a silver mina.

Fortunately, we do have more to go on than that. The Sumerians were obsessive record-keepers and hundreds of tablets of court records called *ditilla* still survive. These tell us that justice was administered on behalf of the king by the *ensi*, the head priest and governor of the individual towns and cities. Temples were used as courtrooms, but only because they provided a convenient place to hold trials. There were no professional judges; they came from all walks of life and were trained at the *adubba*, the temple school, before

TEMPLES WERE USED AS COURTROOMS, BUT ONLY BECAUSE THEY PROVIDED A CONVENIENT PLACE TO HOLD TRIALS.

LEFT: A lithograph from 1852 showing the entrance to the temple, High Mound, Kalhu (Tell Nimrud). Temples were used as court rooms by the Babylonians.

taking up office. Justice was in the hands of the state, but the temple continued to play a role, if only as a source of learning and as a moral witness to the fairness and virtue of the state.

Other elements of the Sumerian legal system are closer to modern practice. Lawsuits could be initiated by private parties and also by the state if it had a vested interest in the case. At trials, evidence consisted of statements made under oath by the parties and by witnesses, and statements or written documents by experts or high officials. Another *ditilla* appears to describe a kind of court of appeals, the 'seven royal judges of Nippur'.

There is a later Sumerian record of a murder trial in which the death penalty was given. The death penalty may have applied for other crimes too, but the majority of offences were punished by fines.

About a century after Ur-Nammu, Lipit-Ishtar, the Amorite Semitic king of

Isin, compiled a legal code in Sumerian, to 'establish justice and care for the well-being of the Sumerians and the Akkadians.' Only part of the text is readable and of that, there are only three legible statutes relating to criminal law. In all cases, the offender is required to pay a fine in compensation:

> If a man entered the orchard of another man and was seized there for stealing, he shall pay ten shekels of silver.

As with the previous Mesopotamian legal codes, the most common punishments are fines.

Laws of Eshunna

After the fall of the Third Dynasty of Ur in 2000 BCE, a number of far-flung new cities were established beyond the original boundaries of Sumer. One of these was Eshunna, 50km (31 miles) north of present-day Baghdad. Not much is known of its history, except that Hammurabi, king of Babylon conquered it in about 1720 BCE.

In 1945 and 1949 two tablets containing the Laws of Eshunna were discovered. They are a loose compilation of statutes, rules and precedents, which have, so far, been only partially deciphered. The author remains unknown and they cannot be attributed to any particular king. The two discovered tablets are thought to be a 'private,' rather than an 'official' copy, possibly owned by court officials or used to teach apprentice scribes.

Eshunnan society had two social classes, the upper-class *awilum* and lower-class *muskenum*. Both classes were free citizens and considered equal under the law. There was also a slave underclass, which had fewer legal rights but was still protected under the law. Surprisingly, a slave could marry an *awilum*, and their children would be born free citizens.

The Laws of Eshunna appear to cover every aspect of civil life, including questions of marriage, divorce, property, loans, inheritance, breach of contract, land disputes and problems with harvests or cattle. In the sections concerning crimes and punishments, the code lists five types of criminal offences: theft and burglary, kidnapping, homicide and bodily injuries, sexual offences, and damages caused to animals.

The punishments mentioned are almost exclusively fines or other forms of compensation. In the case of bodily injury, there is a graded scale of charges:

> If a man bit the nose of a man and severed it, he shall weigh out one mina of silver. An eye – one mina; a tooth, half a mina; an ear – half a mina; a slap in the face – he shall weigh out ten shekels of silver.

There were, however, some capital offences:

A man seized in the crop field of a muskenum in broad daylight shall weigh out ten shekels of silver. [He] seized at night in the crop – he shall die; he shall not live.

Entering a crop field without the authority to do so was considered to be event that preceded theft. As in later ancient legal codes, a distinction is made between the offence when committed in the daytime and the same offence taking place at night. This is because night was associated with sorcery, or at

LEFT: The Ziggurat of Merduk in Babylon, called in Sumerian 'Etemenanki' ('The Foundation of Heaven and Earth'), as imagined by 19th-century French archaeologist Charles Chipiez. After modern quarrying the site is now a large hole.

RIGHT: A Bible illustration by Gustave Doré shows the Hebrews in captivity in Babylon, the prisoners of King Nebuchadnezzar. Hebrew society and beliefs originated in Mesopotamia and continued to be influenced by Mesopotamian thought.

the very least, subterfuge, and any potential threat to the city's food supply was taken extremely seriously.

In some of the statutes, considerable confusion is caused by the fact that the Akkadian language makes no distinction between male and female personal pronouns. Certainly, the code states that one of the guilty parties in an adultery case is to be executed, but it's impossible to be sure if it's the man or the woman:

> The day a woman will be seized in the lap of a man, [he/she] shall die, [he/she] shall not live.

In spite of this syntactical ambiguity, reference to both previous and later punishments suggests that if only one of the offending adulterers was to be punished by execution, it was far more likely to have been the woman rather than the man.

THE CODE OF HAMMURABI

The earliest surviving complete legal code is the Code of Hammurabi, written in Babylon in the Akkadian language in about 1750 BCE. It was widely read and highly influential, serving as a basic template for many later legal codes in Mesopotamia and Europe.

King Hammurabi (1795–1750 BCE) established the power and greatness of the city of Babylon, which at his accession was under the control of the Elamites of western Persia. In the 14th year of his reign, Hammurabi freed his city and then began a series of campaigns against rival city-states. Through a combination of alliances and military campaigns, Hammurabi became by about 1760 BCE the ruler of a united kingdom stretching from the Persian Gulf to the Habur river, roughly the area of modern Iraq and the area known today as the Old Babylonian Empire.

As Hammurabi established his empire, he set about improving its infrastructure and administration. During his reign he personally supervised irrigation, canal building, tax collection, the creation of a postal service and the erection of public buildings. As king, Hammurabi was the head of the judiciary and took his legal responsibilities seriously. Among the thousands of surviving records from his administration are numerous judicial decisions made by Hammurabi and letters of appeal to the king. At the end of his reign Hammurabi unified his empire under a single legal code that has come to be known as the Code of Hammurabi.

The Code was remarkable for introducing legal rights and judicial procedures that have endured to this day, notably, the principle that at least some degree of legal protection is available to all. However, the Code of Hammurabi is known not for its egalitarian principles but for the severity of its punishments. The death penalty is imposed for a wide array of offences and the abiding principle of the Code is the *talio*, the term for sympathetic punishment in which the part of the body that committed the crime is mutilated or amputated.

As with all Mesopotamian legal codes, the Code of Hammurabi begins by proclaiming the greatness of the king:

> That the strong might not injure the weak, in order to protect the widows and orphans, I have in Babylon … in order to declare justice in the land, to settle all disputes, and heal all injuries, set up these my precious words, written upon my memorial stone, before the image of me, as king of righteousness.

> The king who rules among the kings of the cities am I. My words are well considered; there is no wisdom like mine. …Let the oppressed, who have a case

RIGHTS AND FREEDOMS WERE ASSURED IN THE CODE, BUT THEY SEEM MORE OF A BY-PRODUCT OF ITS REAL AIM: TO ENSURE THE WEALTH AND STABILITY OF THE EMPIRE AND THE CONTINUED POWER OF THE RULING ELITE.

RIGHT: The black basalt column upon which the Code of Hammurabi was inscribed in cuneiform writing. At the top of the column is a portrait of Hammurabi, standing before the Babylonian god of justice, Shamash, who is handing the king written laws.

at law, come and stand before this my image as king of righteousness; let him read the inscription, and understand my precious words: the inscription will explain his case to him; he will find out what is just, and his heart will be glad, so that he will say: 'Hammurabi is a ruler, who is as a father to his subjects…'

Hammurabi had the legal code displayed for all to see by having it engraved on a 2m- (6½-ft)high black basalt column and placing it in the temple of Marduk in Babylon. He also erected an unspecified number of copies around the cities of his empire. What is believed to be the original column was found in 1901 by a French archaeological expedition, not in Babylon but in the western Persian city of Susa. It is assumed that the Elamites took the column to their capital city of Susa as a spoil of war when they sacked Babylon in the 12th century BCE. The column is now displayed in the Louvre in Paris.

Naturally, few people could read the statutes, but the bas-relief at the top of the column is an effective piece of pictorial propaganda. It shows Hammurabi, seated on a throne and with his hands raised in prayer, receiving the laws from the sun god, Shamash. Religion is portrayed as subservient to the state, providing a divine justification for state power. This notion of the 'divine right of kings' was one that has persisted long into the modern era.

Law of precedent

The Code itself is not so much a legal code as a compilation of cases and examples reflecting Sumerian customary law and some of Hammurabi's own decisions. Criminal law forms only a part of it. The 282 statutes in 51 columns of cuneiform script were designed to regulate every aspect of Babylonian society, even down to details such as the precise wages of artisans and labourers. Trade, land ownership and agriculture were strictly regulated. Severe penalties were imposed for jeopardizing crops and livestock, and for failure to maintain the canals and dykes of which Hammurabi had built many. Private and family life was well regulated, with statutes concerning marriage, divorce, adoption, inheritance and the ownership of slaves.

Hammurabi brought justice to all his subjects, but not equality. Babylonian society, as in Eshunna, consisted of two free classes, the *awilum* and the *muskenum*, and a slave underclass. Punishment was dispensed entirely according to the status of the victim.

In criminal law, the abiding principle was the *talio*. Assaults among equals were subject to brutally literal sympathetic punishment:

If a man put out the eye of another man, his eye shall be put out. (196)

If he break another man's bone, his bone shall be broken. ... (200)

If a man knock out the teeth of his equal, his teeth shall be knocked out. (196)

A son who struck his father would have his hand cut off, as would a brander who removed an escaped slave's identification mark. Perjury or denying your mother or father was punishable by cutting off your tongue, prying into forbidden secrets by the loss of an eye, and rape was punished by castration.

Lower-class victims were not considered nearly so important, however, and assaulting an inferior would only bring a fine:

If he put out the eye of a freed man, or break the bone of a freed man, he shall pay one gold mina.

If he put out the eye of a man's slave, or break the bone of a man's slave, he shall pay one-half of its value. (196–199)

Private individuals and the state kept slaves; they served in temples, palaces and public buildings and worked on large-scale construction projects. Babylonian slaves consisted of prisoners of war, criminals and debtors. Those who could not pay what they owed were enslaved to their creditors to pay off the debt, or could send their wife or children to serve in their place.

The Code specified that enslaved debtors had to be released when the debt was paid, and could be held no longer than three years. After that, the debt was declared legally forgiven. Criminals could also find themselves enslaved,

'IF A WOMAN QUARREL WITH HER HUSBAND, AND SAY: 'YOU ARE NOT CONGENIAL TO ME,' THE REASONS FOR HER PREJUDICE MUST BE PRESENTED. IF SHE IS GUILTLESS, AND THERE IS NO FAULT ON HER PART, BUT HE LEAVES AND NEGLECTS HER, THEN NO GUILT ATTACHES TO THIS WOMAN, SHE SHALL TAKE HER DOWRY AND GO BACK TO HER FATHER'S HOUSE.' (CODE OF HAMURABI, 142)

striking one's older brother or kicking one's mother were just two crimes so punished.

All slaves, including prisoners of war and those unlucky enough to have been born a slave, had rights under the Code. They were protected from injury and abuse, even from their owners, although their low status is reflected in the fact that even murdering a slave merely carries a fine equal to the cost of replacing the slave with another.

Slaves were paid a salary and were allowed to conduct business and own property. Many slaves were able to eventually purchase their own freedom. They were also allowed to marry free citizens, in which case their children were born free.

Children born to an owner and a female slave were born slaves, but could be, and frequently were, legitimized and adopted by the owner and enjoyed full rights of inheritance. Legitimization and adoption certificates have been found among the Babylonian court records.

Higher up the social ranking than slaves, women in Babylonian society were treated as second-class citizens but did have some legal rights and were treated favourably by the law in some situations. For instance, wives were protected against spousal neglect. If neglect was proved, the marriage was annulled and the wife was allowed to depart with her dowry. A wife accused of adultery by her husband could not be convicted without evidence:

> If a man bring a charge against one's wife, but she is not surprised with another man, she must take an oath and then may return to her house. (131)

Despite this, women's rights still lagged far behind those of men. Wives may have been protected against unsupported accusations of infidelity from their husbands, but if another person brought such an allegation, the wife was forced to undergo a trial by ordeal to prove her innocence:

> If the 'finger is pointed' at a man's wife about another man, but she is not caught sleeping with the other man, she shall jump into the river for her husband. (132)

The suspected adulteress was pitched into the Euphrates. If she were innocent, she would be cast up safely on the other bank. If she were guilty, she would be carried away and drowned.

If a wife failed in her marital duties, her husband could divorce her and send her away without a penny, or else remarry and make her a servant in his house. A husband could divorce a wife who had not borne him children,

'If a state slave or the slave of a freed man marry the daughter of a free man, and children are born, the master of the slave shall have no right to enslave the children of the free.' (130)

though he was required to return her dowry. If a wife had borne children, her husband could not divorce her without paying alimony to support the whole family until all the children were of age. After that, the dowry was divided among the wife and children, and then the wife was free, if she wished, to 'marry the man of her heart.' Divorce was not an option for a woman; if she left the marital home to engage in business she could be divorced and made to forfeit her dowry, and if she was 'a gadabout, … neglecting her house and humiliating her husband.' she was sentenced to death by drowning.

HAMMURABI'S LEGACY

The *talio* does not appear in any legal codes before Hammurabi; earlier Akkadian and Sumerian legal codes had relied on fines and other compensations for offences. Hammurabi followed these earlier models in drawing up his own code, but chose to introduce talionic punishments.

The question remains of why Hammurabi chose to depart from these humane methods of punishment and revert to the more primitive method of vengeance. The answer would seem to be both political and personal. Hammurabi issued his Code in the 40th year of his reign when his empire was at its height. His hard-won empire had been created by a combination of carrot and stick; public works and legal protection on the one hand, and the *talio* and the death penalty on the other.

History showed him that after the death of a charismatic leader, the city-states would begin to reassert their independence and alliances would collapse. Hammurabi probably knew that his empire would not long outlast him, and it is easy to see in Hammurabi's Code an old king's desire to hold on to power and leave something to be remembered by. Hammurabi's empire began to break apart soon after his death, and his empire ended in 1600 BCE when the Hittites invaded Babylon and killed King Samsu-Ditana.

To this day the world quakes at the name of Hammurabi the avenger and marvels at the benevolence of Hammurabi the protector. Hammurabi, 'who conquered the four quarters of the world, made great the name of Babylon', achieved immortality through '… these my precious words, written upon my memorial stone, before the image of me, as king of righteousness'.

A law against rape that is not quite so enlightened as it may appear sums up the status of women:

> If a man violate the betrothed wife of another man, who has never known a man, and still lives in her father's house, and sleep with her and be surprised, this man shall be put to death, but the wife is blameless. (130)

The law is quite specific. It does not protect all girls and women from rape, but merely girls who are already betrothed to be married, and therefore subject to a legal contract that involved a financial transaction. It is this, rather than the person that the law protects.

In other ways, the law did provide a means of protection for its citizens. For example, it attempted to protect people against poor medical treatment, by making physicians accountable for their actions:

> If a physician make a large incision with the operating knife, and kill him, or open a tumour with the operating knife, and cut out the eye, his hands shall be cut off.

The law encouraged doctors to take the utmost care in their work by rewarding them with performance-related pay based on the status of the patient they had treated:

> If he cured a broken bone of an awilum or he has revived his sickness, he will receive five shekels of silver.

> If it is the son of a muskenum, he will receive three shekels of silver.

> If it is the slave of an awilum, he will receive two shekels of silver. (220–222)

The Code also protected its citizens by enumerating the responsibilities of all public officials. The regional governor and city officials were expected to catch criminals, and if they failed to do so they were punished. If they failed to catch a burglar, officials had to replace the stolen property. If a murderer had not been found, officials paid a fine to the victim's relatives.

Even judges were scared into honesty and good conduct by the threat of a large fine and permanent removal from office:

> If a judge try a case, reach a decision, and present his judgment in writing; if later error shall appear in his decision, and it be through his own fault,

'IF A PHYSICIAN MAKE A LARGE INCISION IN THE SLAVE OF A FREED MAN, AND KILL HIM, HE SHALL REPLACE THE SLAVE WITH ANOTHER SLAVE.' (218–219)

then he shall pay twelve times the fine set by him in the case, and he shall be publicly removed from the judge's bench, and never again shall he sit there to render judgement. (5)

If a professional did not do his job properly, he could end up paying the ultimate price. A builder who built a house that fell in and killed its owner could be put to death.

The death penalty

The death penalty was awarded for a vast array of crimes, including theft, selling or receiving stolen goods, kidnapping, assisting fugitive slaves, even for fraudulent sale of drink or keeping a disorderly tavern.

In these cases the manner of death was not stipulated, but many crimes demanded specific forms of execution. Adultery, bigamy, rape of a betrothed maiden or bad conduct as a wife were all punished by drowning, and incest with your mother punished by burning. For burglary, the punishment was hanging, to be carried out on the spot where the crime occurred. The same gruesome symmetry applied to the punishment for theft from a house fire:

> If fire break out in a house, and some one who comes to put it out cast his eye upon the property of the owner of the house, and take the property of the master of the house, he shall be thrown into that self-same fire. (25)

Although the penalties stipulated seem excessively harsh by modern standards, the Code established some important legal principles. Criminals could not be convicted without evidence, witnesses were placed on oath and there were penalties for bringing false accusations. If a plaintiff or witness was proved to have lied in court he was made to suffer the punishment the accused would have been given had he been found guilty – another rather neat piece of talionic symmetry.

Under Babylonian law, citizens also had the right of appeal to a higher court and, ultimately, to the king. Many of the letters to Hammurabi that survive are requests for appeals, some of which he is known to have heard. It was a genuine right and was applied, but one important aim of the Code was to make sure that cases without any merit did not reach the higher courts or the king. Most appeal requests concerned contracts, which is one reason why the Code lays down contract law in such minute detail. With a written code, many frequently recurring matters of dispute could be solved without recourse to a higher court. The appeal court merely had to point to the relevant statute in the Code.

'IF A BUILDER BUILD A HOUSE FOR SOME ONE, AND DOES NOT CONSTRUCT IT PROPERLY, AND THE HOUSE WHICH HE BUILT FALL IN AND KILL ITS OWNER, THEN THAT BUILDER SHALL BE PUT TO DEATH.'

CHAPTER TWO

FROM MOSES
TO MOHAMMED

The Code of Hammurabi was the source of the two other Middle Eastern legal traditions: the Biblical law of the Hebrews and Sharia, the law of Islam. In 70 CE the Romans sacked Jerusalem and though the scholarly tradition of Jewish law continued to evolve it was never again the law of the land. In contrast, though Sharia was intermittently applied and by the mid-20th century had all but died out, it has been reintroduced throughout the Muslim world, given impetus by the political and economic struggles of the developing world.

THE LAW OF MOSES AND THE TEN COMMANDMENTS

As with many ancient peoples, the story of the origins of the Hebrews is a mixture of history, legend and fantasy. According to The Bible, Abraham, the patriarch of the Hebrew tribe, was born in Ur in the time of Hammurabi and emigrated first to Haran in northwestern Mesopotamia and afterwards to Canaan. The origin of the historical Hebrew tribe is uncertain, but they may have been the 'Habiru' frequently mentioned in Mesopotamian cuneiform documents. They are described in these documents as nomads and wanderers and as mercenaries who sold their services to the Babylonians, Assyrians, Hittites and Hurrians.

The Hebrews were one of many Semitic tribes living in Mesopotamia from the earliest times and when they began their conquest of Canaan in about 1500 BCE they continued to absorb Mesopotamian influences from the Canaanite population. Egyptian thought and society also influenced the Hebrews long before Egypt's 40-year rule of Canaan in the reign of Ramses II (d. *c.*1225 BCE). In about 1730 BCE the Hebrews had joined a loose confederation of Semitic tribes called the Hyskos. Together they migrated south into Egypt and took control, ruling for 180 years before being

LEFT: This illustration dating from 1920 depicts the Biblical character Simeon in prison.

overthrown in a rebellion. The Hebrews were placed in bondage until Moses led the mass Exodus back to their homeland. It was during this long migration, while wandering in the Sinai desert, that Moses is said to have received the Ten Commandments.

The Biblical account of the Hebrews' return to Canaan relates the sacking of Jericho and the bloody massacre of all the Canaanites, but the archaeological evidence does not support this. Rather, the Hebrews appear to have gradually spread through the land, replacing the dwindling Canaanite population as they established their nation.

The Egyptians did not quickly forget the insult to their authority that the Exodus represented. The Egyptian historian Manetho, writing in the third century BCE, spoke of the 'people from the East' who 'subdued Egypt, by stratagem and force, only to be driven out subsequently in ignominy, before making their way to the land of Judea. Here they established their capital, Jerusalem, and adopted a law code based on the hatred of all humankind except their own.'

According to the Biblical Book of Exodus, in about 1300 BCE Moses received, directly from God, two stone tablets bearing probably the most famous set of laws ever written. The Ten Commandments and their basic tenets are today enshrined in legal codes throughout the world:

The Ten Commandments are an efficient summary of a citizen's duties under the law, but without mention of punishment they do not constitute a legal code. There are, however, extensive lists of crimes and punishments throughout the first five books of The Bible, known as the Torah ('Law'). Biblical punishments follow Hammurabi in employing sympathetic punishment. This suited the simple classless structure of Hebrew society because it did not distinguish between rich and poor. According to their religious doctrine, every Israelite was considered freeborn. Sympathetic punishment was also employed because it was considered the best deterrent:

> And all Israel shall hear and fear, and shall do not more any such wickedness in the midst of Thee.
>
> (*The Bible*, Deuteronomy, 13:12)

The influence of the Code of Hammurabi on the Biblical laws is clear; they share much of the same structure, content and terminology. They also both have a basis in religion. Hammurabi claims in the introduction to his code to have been called upon by the gods to establish justice in his kingdom. In frequent utterances such as: 'My words which I have inscribed on my monument' and: 'The judgements that I have judged' he stamps his

BIBLICAL LAWS STATE A DIRECT LINK WITH GOD, CLAIMING TO BE 'WRITTEN WITH THE FINGER OF GOD'. EVERY CRIME IS THEREFORE A VIOLATION OF GOD'S WILL AND MUST BE PUNISHED.

THE TEN COMMANDMENTS

And God spake all these words, saying, I am the Lord thy God, which have brought thee out of the land of Egypt, out of the house of bondage.

1. Thou shalt have no other gods before me.
2. Thou shalt not make unto thee any graven image, or any likeness of any thing that is in heaven above, or that is in the earth beneath, or that is in the water under the earth:
   Thou shalt not bow down thyself to them, nor serve them: for I the Lord thy God am a jealous God, visiting the iniquity of the fathers upon the children unto the third and fourth generation of them that hate me;
   And shewing mercy unto thousands of them that love me, and keep my commandments.
3. Thou shalt not take the name of the Lord thy God in vain; for the Lord will not hold him guiltless that taketh his name in vain.
4. Remember the Sabbath day, to keep it holy. Six days shalt thou labour, and do all thy work: but the seventh day is the Sabbath of the Lord thy God: in it thou shalt not do any work, thou, nor thy son, nor thy daughter, thy manservant, nor thy maidservant, nor thy cattle, nor thy stranger that is within thy gates: for in six days the Lord made heaven and earth, the sea, and all that in them is, and rested the seventh day: wherefore the Lord blessed the sabbath day, and hallowed it.
5. Honour thy father and thy mother: that thy days may be long upon the land which the Lord thy God giveth thee.
6. Thou shalt not kill.
7. Thou shalt not commit adultery.
8. Thou shalt not steal.
9. Thou shalt not bear false witness against thy neighbour.
10. Thou shalt not covet thy neighbour's house, thou shalt not covet thy neighbour's wife, nor his manservant, nor his maidservant, nor his ox, nor his ass, nor any thing that is thy neighbour's.

(The Bible, Exodus 20: 1–17)

authorship on the codes. The Biblical laws, however, state a direct link with God, claiming to be 'written with the finger of God'. Every crime was therefore a violation of God's will and must be punished. The difference in the Babylonian and Jewish concepts of law is shown by their attitudes to murder.

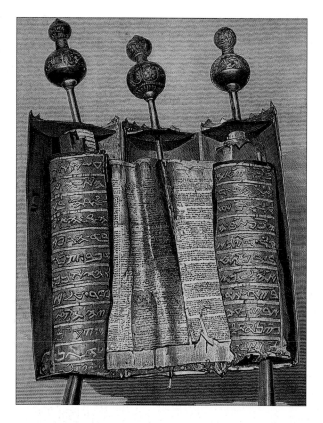

ABOVE: An ancient
Palestinian scroll of the
first five books of the Bible,
known as the Torah to the
Jews. The Torah contains
the Hebrew laws but is
supplemented by other
written and oral sources.

Under the Mesopotamian codes, the victim's family could accept monetary compensation, but under Jewish law a convicted murderer had to be executed.

Despite the claim of literal divine authorship, the Jewish laws were a collective enterprise. Unknown authors wrote the Torah in around the third century BCE and although it is a central text, it is only one element of the corpus of Jewish law, called the Halacha. The Halacha consists not only of written law, but also of statements handed down by tradition, oral law, sayings of elders and scribes, and customs.

The legal tenets of the Torah were complemented by interpretations of the Mishnah (the oral law), and the Talmud, an encyclopaedic compilation of legal debates, history, folk tales, proverbs and dialogues. The Mishnah was compiled and edited by Rabbi Judah ha-Nasi by the end of the second century BCE, and the Talmud was compiled between 220 BCE and 470 CE. The tradition of analysis and interpretation did not end there; both the Cordoban philosopher Maimonides (1135–1204) and Joseph ben Ephraim Caro (1488–1575) made significant codifications and re-interpretations of Mishnaic and Talmudic law.

Punishments

Punishments in Jewish legal philosophy serve three purposes. They are retributive (punishing the criminal for his act), deterrent (severe enough to intimidate others from committing the crime) and expiatory (attempting to obtain God's forgiveness).

Imprisonment, banishment, sympathetic punishment, flagellation and fines punished non-capital crimes. Imprisonment was reserved for repeat offenders who had been convicted twice before. According to Maimonides, imprisonment was used for those who had committed a capital crime but could not be executed because of a technicality. Those who had hired an assassin to commit a murder were also imprisoned, since Biblical and Talmudic law restricted the death sentence to those who carried it out.

For unintentional homicide or manslaughter, the penalty was banishment to one of six designated cities of refuge. Banishment abroad was not considered as the offender could be forced to worship foreign gods. Banishment lasted until death of the city's high priest. If the high priest died a week after an offender was banished, the offender would be set free, but if a young and healthy high priest had just been appointed, the offender would probably spend his life in captivity. Prisoners were housed at the city's expense as they were living there against their will. They were fed and clothed by the high priest's family – presumably to ensure the high priest did not come to an untimely end. Cities of refuge also provided asylum for accused criminals who needed protection against lynching by the victim's family. If a convincing case was presented against the fugitive he was then extradited, under protective guard, to face trial.

Offences against the person were punished by sympathetic punishment; the offender received the same injury that he had inflicted on his victim:

> Life for life,
> Eye for eye, tooth for tooth, hand for hand, foot for foot,
> Burning for burning, wound for wound, stripe for stripe.
>
> (*The Bible*, Exodus 21:23)

BELOW: 'The crushing one to pieces under stones'. This Biblical punishment involved covering the victims in thorns and placing large boulders on them to crush them.

RIGHT: The death of St Stephen in Jerusalem, 35 CE. The first Christian to die for his faith, Stephen was charged with blasphemy, tried before the Sanhedrin and sentenced to death by stoning.

In the post-Biblical period, commentators began to interpret these words metaphorically, as 'the value of' an eye, hand or foot, preferring fines as compensation for bodily injury.

Flogging was the preferred punishment for a total of 168 offences, including seven types of incest, eight violations of dietary laws, three violations of marital laws by priests, marrying a bastard or a descendant of the Gibeonites, and having sex with a menstruating woman.

The Bible states:

> Forty stripes he may give him, and not exceed: lest, if he should exceed, and beat him above these with many stripes, then thy brother should seem vile unto thee.
>
> (*The Bible*, Deuteronomy 25:2–3)

In post-Biblical times the number of stripes was reduced to 39 so that even if there were an error in counting, the total would never exceed 40. Later,

Talmudic scholars introduced the concept of flogging a man 'according to his strength'; this meant that he would receive only as many lashes as the court thought he could bear.

Under Biblical law, fines were reserved for property crimes and minor bodily injuries. The Mesopotamian codes had punished robbery under certain conditions with the death penalty, but under the Hebrew laws, theft was never punished by death. Punishment could also be avoided if the offender confessed his guilt and repented.

Debtors were sold into bondage to pay off their debts but were freed as soon as their debts were paid, and could not serve more than six years of slavery:

> If thou buy an Hebrew servant, six years he shall serve: and in the seventh he shall go out free for nothing.
>
> (*The Bible*, Exodus 21:2)

Capital crimes

Mosaic law defines 36 capital crimes, including murder, sexual offences, idolatry, blasphemy and desecration of the Sabbath. Witchcraft was also a capital crime, prohibited by the words 'Thou shalt not suffer a witch to live,' which were later to have such dire consequences in Europe and New England.

The Bible lists three methods of execution. These are stoning, burning and decapitation. Stoning was the most common method, used mainly for crimes that affected the wellbeing of the whole community, including sex crimes. Stoning was carried out collectively, but the prosecuting witnesses were required to cast the first stones. It was thought that the heavy responsibility of carrying out the execution would deter witnesses from making false accusations.

Death by burning was the punishment for nine categories of incest and one of adultery – that of sex with a married daughter of a priest. The method of burning is not clear, but a 'humane' method was used in post-Biblical times. The condemned was strangled, using a rope held at either end by the two witnesses. The rope was covered with soft material so as not to cause the condemned additional pain by scratching his neck. When the condemned opened his mouth, molten lead was poured down his throat, burning his internal organs.

Considered the quickest and most humane of methods decapitation was reserved for wilful murderers and those convicted of communal apostasy (the renunciation of religion). Whenever Mosaic law did not stipulate the method of execution, the Talmud determined that the condemned should be

'AND IT SHALL BE, IF THE WICKED MAN BE WORTHY TO BE BEATEN, THAT THE JUDGE SHALL CAUSE HIM TO LIE DOWN, AND TO BE BEATEN BEFORE HIS FACE, ACCORDING TO HIS FAULT, BY A CERTAIN NUMBER.' (EXODUS, 22:3)

RIGHT: Mohammed ibn Abdullah, born in Mecca in 570, united the Arab people under a new religion and founded the Islamic Arab empire. His teachings, as recorded in the Koran and other sources, are the foundation of Sharia law.

strangled. This applied to crimes including wounding one's father or mother, kidnapping an Israelite, false prophecy, and falsely accusing a priest's daughter of adultery. It was also applied to a 'rebellious judge' – one who refused to acknowledge the authority of the appeal court, the Great Sanhedrin, in overturning one of his decisions.

The Biblical code may have been harsh, but Jewish judicial practices favoured mercy and embodied some important legal rights, including equality before the law and protection against self-incrimination – 'ein adam meisim atzmo rasha' ('a man cannot declare himself wicked.'). Guilt could only be determined by evidence and a person confessing a crime without evidence was not to be believed. No case could be brought without the testimony of at least two competent witnesses.

The harsh Biblical penalties may have been carried out to the letter at one time, but certainly by Mishnaic times courts favoured a lenient interpretation of the law. Stoning, for example, was replaced by the quicker method of simply pushing the prisoner off a ledge. Stone hitting a person's body was the same as a person's body hitting stone ran the argument. 'Stoning houses' were constructed using a ledge placed at twice the height of a man, as it was determined that this height would kill the man but not do him the indignity of mutilating his body. If the condemned was not killed, a heavy stone was dropped on his chest to kill him quickly. As with conventional stonings, the prosecution witnesses carried out the execution.

Perhaps because Jewish law was seen as the law of God, great care was taken to avoid convicting the innocent. A defendant could not be found guilty unless he was warned when committing the crime that what he was about to do was illegal and what the likely penalty would be. If this condition was met, there were numerous safeguards built in to judicial procedure. In all trials, witnesses' testimony was considered as a unit, rather than individually, so if one witness's testimony among many was dubious, the case was dismissed.

There were further safeguards in capital cases. Capital cases had to be tried by at least 23 judges, who needed a majority of at least two to convict. Trial and sentencing normally took place in a single day, but in capital cases, sentence could not be passed until the next day to give the judges time to reconsider. They could change their minds only from a guilty to a not guilty verdict; a not guilty verdict could not be overturned. When voting in capital cases, the normal order of precedence was reversed. Junior judges voted first so that they were not influenced by the decisions of their seniors.

The rules regarding executions contained further built-in safeguards. The site of execution was placed far from the court to allow as much time as possible between sentencing and execution. Judges were not allowed to join

MOHAMMED BEGAN PREACHING THAT ALLAH WAS THE ONLY GOD, THAT ALL BELIEVERS WERE EQUAL BEFORE HIM, THAT THE RICH MUST SHARE THEIR WEALTH WITH THE POOR, AND THAT A DAY OF JUDGEMENT WOULD COME.

the execution procession, but remained in court to reconsider the evidence. If one of them felt he had a new argument that cast doubt on the judgement, the procession was stopped and the prisoner returned to court. There was also a herald at the head of the execution procession calling for anyone with information that could save the condemned to come forward. If a member of the public stepped forward, the condemned was returned and the new witness's evidence heard.

THE LAW OF ISLAM

The Arabian peninsula has been occupied since prehistory by a variety of mostly Semitic tribes, known since the first centuries CE as the Arabs. The Arab tribes, mostly based in villages, were more often than not in conflict with one another, but from time to time theocratic governments grew up and brought a short-lived unity. The Arabian peninsula was criss-crossed by trade routes and there were permanent contacts with Egyptian, European and Indo-Persian civilizations, but the relative isolation of the interior of the peninsula helped to preserve its distinctive cultural and religious practices.

The Arab economy was based on agriculture, fishing and trade, especially of frankincense. Two of the four known early Arab kingdoms, Ma'in and Saba showed clear Mesopotamian influences in their social structure. Ma'in had a structure similar to that of a Mesopotamian city-state, being ruled by a king with a cabinet of counsellors and magistrates. Ruled by priest-kings who combined religious and temporal power, Saba was similar to an earlier Mesopotamian model.

Arabia eventually became the cradle of Islam, which remains essentially Arab in its outlook, despite later influences as it spread. Islam is an inherently conservative religion that requires total obedience to God and Islamic law – the word 'islam' means 'submitting' or 'surrendering'. Changes in the law are not sanctioned unless they are seen as a return to the purity of the original law. Islamic law began with the founder of Islam, Mohammed.

In about 570, Mohammed ibn Abdullah was born in Mecca into a branch of the aristocratic Quraysh clan. With no fortune of his own, Mohammed entered the world of business and became a successful commercial agent in the caravan trade. Mohammed frequently travelled with the caravan to Syria, then a part of the Christian Byzantine Empire. A number of Arabs in Mohammed's time had converted to Christianity and there were tribes of Arabian Jews. There were also the Hanifs, followers of the prophet Abraham who worshipped the same God as the Jews and Christians. The spiritual ideas Mohammed encountered evidently had an effect on him, and he began to speak out against the extremes of wealth and poverty he saw around him in

'FINALLY THE OUTLINES AND MANY DETAILS OF ISLAMIC LAW WERE CAST INTO THE FORM OF TRADITIONS FROM THE PROPHET. IN THIS WAY, ONE OF THE GREATEST AND MOST SUCCESSFUL OF LITERARY FICTIONS CAME INTO BEING.' (JOSEPH SCHACHT, *THE CAMBRIDGE HISTORY OF ISLAM*)

Mecca. In 610, Mohammed saw a vision of the angel Gabriel (Jabril in Arabic), who told him: 'Thou art the apostle of God.' From 610 until his death in 632, Mohammed received the divine revelations that would be compiled by his followers into the Koran, which was completed some ten or 20 years after Mohammed's death.

Mohammed began preaching that Allah was the only god, that all believers were equal before him, that the rich must share their wealth with the poor, and that a day of judgement would come. The new religion, which Mohammed early on began calling Islam, was a synthesis of the two monotheistic religions of Judaism and Christianity, but with a unique and distinctly Arab dimension. Allah was an Arabic god, and to claim equal status with the Judaeo-Christian god was a political statement in itself. Islam was from its beginnings a political movement as well as a religious one, and always one that attracted the poor and disenfranchised.

ABOVE: An 1853 engraving from British explorer Richard Burton's book *Pilgrimage to Mecca and Medina*, showing pilgrims stoning the 'great devil.'

ABOVE: A sign outside the higher Sharia court in the Nigerian city of Gusauthe, the state of Zamfara, demonstrates the adherence to Sharia law. Zamfara transformed Nigerian politics in 2000 when it extended Sharia from the civil law to criminal law in establishing severe punishments for adultery.

The Meccan authorities considered Mohammed's ideas dangerous and began a campaign of persecution against him and his multitude of followers. In September 622, they left Mecca for Yathrib. Mohammed's flight to Yathrib, the *hejira*, is traditionally taken as the beginning of the Islamic era. It was in Yathrib (later called Medina) that Mohammed established Islam as a political entity and created a revolutionary militia that was to sweep all before it.

Years of sporadic skirmishes with the Meccans followed and early victories swelled the ranks of Mohammed's followers, until in 630, the Islamic forces captured Mecca. Mohammed entered the Kaaba in triumph, destroying the pagan gods and establishing the site as the spiritual site of Islam.

SHARIA

… then we gave you a Sharia in religion, follow it, and do not follow the lust of those who do not know.

(*Koran*, 40: 17)

Sharia, which means 'clear path' or 'highway', is the law of the Islamic world. In Islam, as in Judaism, law is considered to be of divine origin and governs ritual, belief and actions down to the last details of daily life. The Islamic conception of law is entirely authoritarian. Law is the will of God as revealed through the Prophet and, therefore, breaking the law is an act of religious disobedience.

Law is part of a theology that regulates all human actions. In the Islamic system, there are five classes of actions:

1) Obligations, such as praying or giving alms (*zakah*).
2) Desirable or recommended actions, such as freeing slaves or giving alms to beggars.
3) Indifferent or morally neutral actions, such as going on a pleasure trip.
4) Objectionable but not forbidden actions, such as gambling, marking the Koran or eating onion or garlic, which cause bad breath.
5) Prohibited actions (*haram*), such as murder or drinking alcohol.

(Israel Drapkin, *Crime and Punishment in the Ancient World*)

> SHARIA DOES NOT PUNISH THE PLANNING OF A CRIME, ONLY THE CRIME ITSELF, BUT THERE APPEARS TO BE AN EXCEPTION IN THE CASE OF ATTEMPTED COUP D'ÉTAT, THOUGH IN THIS MATTER, TOO, THERE ARE DIVERGENT SCHOOLS OF THOUGHT.

Sharia is based primarily on the Koran, which, as the revealed word of God, contains the most perfect solutions to questions of morality and conduct. But as it is relatively short and contains few direct references to law, the Koran is supplemented by other sources. The first of these are the *sunna*, the works of the Prophet, which include a compilation of sayings attributed to him that are called the *hadith*. Other sources are *kias*, which are analogy based on previous decisions, and *ijma*, the consensus of jurists and religious scholars throughout the Muslim community.

Sharia, in other words, was created by Islamic jurists in the first two centuries of Islam, and like other legal codes, Sharia was a means of formalizing the practices of state law and power. Islam underwent a rapid expansion and by the time of Mohammed's death it had spread throughout most of Arabia. A century later, *dar-al-Islam* (the lands of Islam) extended to North Africa and Spain and throughout the Middle East as far as Central Asia and India.

In the seventh century, the great Umayyad dynasty (661–750 CE) based in Damascus was the dominant power in the Islamic world. It was during the

Umayyad period that the process of formalizing Sharia was completed. The theory and practice of Sharia varied widely throughout Islam according to local social and legal practices, and four main schools of law grew up, each with their own interpretations. As the jurists searched for a theoretical justification for their decisions based on current practice, they began to ascribe their decisions to the authority of past figures – the first caliphs (the rulers who succeeded Mohammed), the 'Companions of the Prophet', and ultimately, the Prophet himself.

As Joseph Schacht writes in *The Cambridge History of Islam*:

> In Iraq, very early in the eighth century, when the term 'Sunna of the Prophet' was transferred from its political and theological into a legal context. … This term … did not as yet imply the existence of positive information in the form

DISCRETIONARY PUNISHMENTS (*TA'ZIR*)

Discretionary punishments are for those offences that are not *hadd* and not punishable by retaliation. The punishments were established during the Ummayad dynasty and were intended to cover new offences not listed in the `Koran. Punishments were originally established by analogy with offences in the Koran or *sunnah*, or traced to the opinions of Mohammed or his successors.

The many *ta'zir* offences include eating prohibited items such as blood or corpses, perjury, usury, slander, stealing minor items, accepting bribes, selling short weights or measures, and espionage on behalf of a non-Muslim enemy. The judge has considerable leeway in determining the level of punishment for each crime, often in the absence of a comprehensive legal code. Punishments vary widely, from counselling or private admonition, censure in court or public denunciation, to suspended sentences, fines, exile, flogging, imprisonment and, for offences such as espionage, death.

Evidentiary standards are less rigorous than for *hadd* offences: either a confession or the testimony of two witnesses. Some jurists even allow one of the witnesses to be a woman; for *hadd* offences the witnesses must all be men. Confessions of *ta'zir* crimes cannot be rescinded and some jurists even believe that a judge may convict purely on his own knowledge, without the need for either a confession or witnesses.

of the 'Traditions' (Hadith), that the Prophet by his words or acts had in fact originated or approved any particular practice. It was not long before these Traditions, too, came into existence…

After the authority of the Prophet himself had been invoked by identifying the established doctrine with his *sunna*, a more specific reference to him was needed, and there appeared detailed statements or 'Traditions' which claimed to be the reports of ear- or eye-witnesses of the words or acts of the Prophet, handed down orally by an uninterrupted chain of trustworthy persons….

Some of the *hadith* no doubt have a claim to authenticity, but many, perhaps most, do not. In the eighth century, as today, state and religious power élites claimed a scriptural authority for the exercise of power, a scriptural authority that could not be denied – under Islam, the ultimate authority is to the Koran and the words and example of the Prophet.

The fixing of Sharia was completed in the era of the next great Muslim empire: the Abbasid dynasty based in Baghdad (750–1258). Whenever the learned scholars of Islam reached agreement on a point, their decision was considered irrevocable and no further debate was permitted. The right of personal interpretation of the law, *itjihad*, was permitted only on points not yet decided upon. In the 12th century, the jurists considered all the debates answered and declared that 'the gates of *itjihad* are closed.' As Schacht states: 'Islamic law reached its full development in early Abbasid times, and its institutions reflect the social and economic conditions of Islamic society of that period more than any other.'

Crimes and punishments

According to Sharia, a crime is defined as a legally forbidden and punishable act, or the omission of a duty that is commanded. The basic principle is that everything is permitted (*halal*) unless specifically prohibited or discouraged.

Sharia classifies offences by the types of punishments they attract:

1) Those with a specific punishment (*hadd*).
2) Those whose punishment is at the judge's discretion (*ta'zir*).
3) Those deserving retaliatory action (*kisas*) inflicted by the victim's family, or blood money (*diya*) paid by the offender or his family.
4) Those against the policy of the state, deserving administrative penalties (*siyasa*).
5) Those that are corrected by acts of personal penance or expiation (*kaffara*).

The first three categories of offences are heard before a *qadi*, a judge of a juryless Sharia court. Secular courts handle administrative penalties, and *kaffara* is undertaken voluntarily and is, therefore, considered outside the sphere of the court.

Specified punishments (**hadd**)

These are fixed punishments specified in the Koran and hadith for the crimes of adultery and unlawful intercourse (*zina*), defamation and false accusation, drinking alcohol, theft, highway robbery, apostacy from Islam, and attempted coup d'état. Also related are crimes punishable by *talio* and blood money, such as murder (whether premeditated, semi-premeditated or by error) and premeditated serious assault.

Zina includes intercourse with anyone who is not your legal spouse or concubine, such as a close relative, a prostitute, a girl before the age of puberty,

BELOW: In 1998 a videotape was smuggled out of Iran claiming to document a public stoning for the first time, an execution carried out at a Revolutionary Guard barracks in 1991. The Iranian government said the video was a fake.

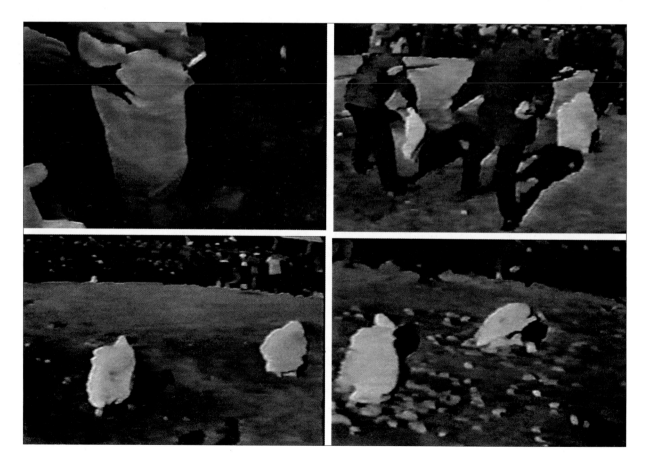

or a fifth wife if you have four living wives. Adultery is not legal grounds for divorce, but it is considered an offence against God. The punishment for *zina* is death by stoning for a free person who has been convicted. For all others, the punishment is 100 lashes or 50 for a slave. These punishments are not mentioned in the Koran, but were inflicted by the first caliphs.

Because of the severity of the punishment there are very strict evidentiary requirements: the accusation must be brought within a month of the offence, there must be four male witnesses instead of the normal two, or the accused must confess to the crime. Some jurists have even considered that it is meritorious for the witnesses not to testify, leaving the offender to atone for the offence privately with God. Witnesses are also constrained by the more practical consideration that if the accusation is dismissed, even for technical reasons, they are subject to the *hadd* punishment for false accusation of adultery: 80 lashes for free persons and 40 lashes for slaves.

Drinking alcohol is punished by 80 lashes for a free person and 40 lashes for a slave. Prohibition of drinking was imposed by Mohammed, who was outraged by the drunkenness of his fellow Arabs which he felt was harmful to the fabric of society. The punishment is not mentioned in the Koran but was established later.

Theft is punished by the amputation of a hand. For a second conviction, the left foot is amputated, for a third, the right foot, and for a fourth, the left hand. There are several limitations to the application of the punishment; the accused must be a competent adult, the theft must be intentional and performed by stealth. The *hadd* punishment does not apply to pickpockets or to a thief apprehended before he has left the victim's home. The stolen goods must be of a set minimum value, and the stolen item must be a legal one; there is no *hadd* punishment for the theft of wine. The theft of books is exempt; under Sharia there are no intellectual property rights and it is assumed that the thief has stolen the book for its contents rather than for the book itself.

Highway robbery or brigandage is considered a serious offence that threatens social stability. The offences covered in this category are the robbery of travellers far from home and armed entrance into a private house with

DISCRETIONARY ADMINISTRATIVE PENALTIES (*SIYASA*)

The state cannot legislate independently from the Sharia, but it may enforce administrative regulations that are not covered by Sharia. *Siyasa* regulations are intended not to conflict with Sharia laws, but in practice from the earliest years of the rise of Islam they became a means for the state to supplant Sharia laws with their own. This was easiest to achieve in the ill-defined category of discretionary *ta'zir* punishments.

There is leeway within the Sharia legal tradition for state control of the law; jurists have recognized the right of secular courts to limit the jurisdiction of Sharia judges. By the mid-20th century, many Islamic states had adopted secular criminal codes and either abolished Sharia courts or restricted them to areas outside criminal law, before the resurgence of Sharia at the end of the century.

RIGHT: Jamshidieh Park, Tehran, October 27 2002 – a police cameraman records video footage of the hanging of murderer Hashem Anbarniya. In Iran the death penalty is usually reserved for murder, rape, armed robbery and drug trafficking.

intent to rob. Punishment is severe: the amputation of the right hand and left foot, and for a second offence, the left hand and right foot. If the offender also killed the victim, the punishment is beheading with the sword, or if the killing was premeditated, the punishment is crucifixion with the stipulation that the body must be left to hang for three days. The death sentence is mandatory and cannot be redeemed by payment of blood money.

Apostasy from Islam consists of renouncing Islam by word or deed, worshipping other gods, rejecting the Islamic commandments or defaming the Prophet, the angels or the Koran. These acts are considered detrimental to the faith of other Muslims and the penalty is death. Some schools of Islam have held that the offender can be killed with impunity without the need for a trial. However, others do not consider apostasy a *hadd* offence at all, and some modern jurists claim that the penalty has no authority from any sources.

Talio (kisas) and blood money (diya)

As in other societies before centralized government and written laws, in pre-Islamic Arabia, attacks on the clan were punished by the clan and blood feuds were common. As in Homeric Greece, there were courts of arbitration which attempted to replace unrestricted clan vengeance with talionic punishment of the offender or the payment of blood money to the victim's clan.

Islamic law abolished the blood feud and placed limits on vengeance. A trial to determine guilt was necessary before any act of vengeance and punishments were determined by law, according to the degree of culpability of the offender and the degree of harm inflicted on the victim.

Sharia stipulates three kinds of punishment for homicide or bodily harm: retaliation, blood money and penitence. In cases punished by retaliation, the offender suffers the same fate as the victim. For bodily injuries, this means exact retribution – an eye for an eye, a tooth for a tooth. However, there is no retaliation for the loss of an organ of which there is only one, such as a nose or a penis. In that case the victim must accept blood money.

In homicide cases, the victim's next of kin carries out the punishment and in cases of bodily harm, the victim is entitled to carry out the punishment. Punishment is carried out by a state executioner today, and it appears that this was often the case even in the first centuries of Islam. If the victim had no family, the state brought the prosecution.

Homicide or wounding can also be punished by the payment of blood money (*diya*). According to eighth-century Arabian custom, the traditional diya was set at two levels: for serious and for lesser crimes. The heavy *diya* was 100 female camels, with equal numbers of one-, two-, three- and four-year-old animals; the light *diya* was 80 female camels of the same age ranges, plus 20 one-year-old male camels.

The full *diya* is due only to free male Muslims. The diya for a woman is half that of a man, for a male non-Muslim the *diya* varies from a third to a half and for a slave the *diya* is his market value. There is a scale of punishments for bodily harm: the loss of a unique organ receives the same *diya* as for homicide. There are proportionately smaller payments for organs of which there is more than one: half for an arm, leg or eye, one-tenth for a finger, one-thirtieth for each joint of a finger and one-twentieth for a tooth.

Acts of penitence (kaffara)

Acts of *kaffara* include freeing a Muslim slave, fasting during the daylight hours, abstaining from sex or giving to the poor. Kaffara is almost always voluntary, but in rare cases a judge may require it. Offences punished by kaffara include breaking an oath, perjury, breaking fast during Ramadan or violating religious regulations during a pilgrimage to Mecca.

ISLAM AFTER MOHAMMED

From the 10th century, the Abbasid empire declined, weakened by internal rivalries and then defeated by the Christian Crusaders. The Mongol invasion of the 13th century brought the Abbasid caliphate to an end, leaving a power

DRINKING ALCOHOL IS PUNISHED BY 80 LASHES FOR A FREE PERSON AND 40 LASHES FOR A SLAVE. PROHIBITION OF DRINKING WAS IMPOSED BY MOHAMMED, WHO WAS OUTRAGED BY THE DRUNKENNESS OF HIS FELLOW ARABS WHICH HE FELT WAS HARMFUL TO THE FABRIC OF SOCIETY.

vacuum in the Islamic world that would eventually be filled by the rise of the Turkish Ottoman Empire. The Ottomans took Constantinople from the Byzantines in 1453, renaming it Istanbul, and by the 16th century they controlled much of the Middle East and North Africa. Arabs remained under Ottoman control for the next 300 years.

The rise of European colonialism in the 19th and 20th centuries heralded the decline of the Ottoman Empire. At the beginning of World War I, North Africa was under the control of France (Morocco, Tunisia, Algeria), Italy (Libya) or Britain (Egypt). The war finally ended the Ottoman Empire and its remaining Arab territories were divided between Britain and France. Iraq and Palestine went to Britain, and Syria and Lebanon were conceded to France.

The brief of both the British and French mandates stipulated a move towards Arab self-determination, but it was not forthcoming. Arab resentment grew, focused by the granting of much of Palestine to the burgeoning Zionist movement and the creation of the state of Israel in 1948; the British had formerly suggested that Palestine would be one of the lands given over to Arab self-rule.

Arab nations gained their independence in stages after World War II, some peacefully and some, including Algeria, after many years of bitter revolutionary struggle. Almost without exception, the postwar Arab governments were secular. Although many leaders, such as Egypt's Gamal Abdel Nasser, were pan-Arab nationalists who believed in the creation of a single Arab state, they all shared a devotion to westernization and modernization. Sharia courts were relegated to the realm of personal status and secular constitutions were introduced.

Throughout the Arab world, the post-colonial legacy proved traumatic. Secular governments failed to deliver their promises of economic prosperity and national stability. Undemocratic and repressive regimes widened the gap between rich and poor and the newly independent nations were soon heavily in debt, diverting funds for much-needed development to pay off loans. The young, in particular, began to question the Western social and economic policies of their often corrupt governments. Many turned to Islam as a means of restoring their national strength and self-respect, envisaging a return to the glories of the Arab past. This modern Islamic movement had started as early as 1929, with the formation of the Muslim Brotherhood in Egypt.

Islam in the 20th century

The Islamic reform movements of the 20th century took some of their inspiration from the strict interpretation of Islam imposed by the Saudi religious élite in Saudi Arabia. 'Wahhabism', the severe brand of Islam practised in Saudi Arabia, originated in the 18th century as a movement for Islamic purity led by Muhammad ibn Abd al-Wahhab (1703–91) in opposition to the decadent and irreligious practices of the rulers. In alliance with the Saud family, the Wahhabis conquered virtually the whole of Arabia by 1811, establishing their capital at Riyadh. After being pushed out by the Ottoman sultan, who was nominally in charge of Arabia, the Wahhabis finally rose again when Abd al-Aziz ibn Saud recaptured Riyadh in 1902. In 1932 he founded the modern state of Saudi Arabia and reclaimed most of his ancestral territories. The Saudi interpretation of Islam includes the prohibition of the sale and consumption of alcohol, strict sexual segregation, the ban of women driving and many other social restrictions.

BELOW: Nigeria, August 19, 2002: Amina Lawal's legal defence team at the Sharia court of appeal. The appeal court upheld the sentence of death by stoning passed on Lawal in March for the crime of adultery.

Some Islamic groups advocated reform, others violent revolution, but after the loss of territory to Israel in 1967, the mood turned more militant. In the 1970s, the mostly Arab OPEC (Organization of Petroleum Exporting Countries) was a galvanizing force for regional economic and political power that moved to quadruple oil prices in 1973. Arab states – at least those with oil

– began to realize the power of controlling the world's oil supply; about a quarter of the world's oil reserves lies under the Saudi Arabian desert.

However, it was the Islamic revolution of (non-Arab) Iran in 1979 that provided a model for revival movements and the present reintroduction of Sharia throughout the Islamic world. Iran's ruler, Muhammad Reza Shah Pahlavi, pursued a pro-Western policy of economic modernization, enriching himself and the country's elite with new-found oil wealth but doing little for the poor and marginalized mass of the population. In 1979, a popular uprising deposed him and installed the Shi'ite clerical 'mullocracy' led by Ayatollah Ruhollah Khomeini.

In most Muslim states, Sharia has always existed as a moral and spiritual guide, but in the 20th and early 21st centuries it was reintroduced as law in countries including Saudi Arabia, the Gulf States, Iran, Iraq, Pakistan and Yemen. It has been partially reintroduced in Nigeria and Sudan and there are powerful movements for its reintroduction in Bangladesh and Indonesia. The reintroduction of Sharia not only marks a religious revival, but a political one that is very much a part of the post-colonial rise of Arab nationalism and Third World radicalism.

IN COUNTRIES THAT HAVE UNDERGONE AN ISLAMIC REVIVAL, SHARIA IS APPLIED STRICTLY, AND PUNISHMENTS SUCH AS AMPUTATIONS AND STONING ARE REGULARLY APPLIED.

In countries that have undergone an Islamic revival, Sharia is applied strictly, and punishments such as amputations and stoning are regularly applied. The divine origin of the Koran and *sunnah* are invoked as a justification for the strict application of penalties, in an attempt to recreate the perceived purity of an Islamic past. Sudan introduced Sharia in 1983, and within two months sent a delegation (including an orthopaedic surgeon) to Saudi Arabia to learn about the judicial and medical procedures for amputation. In the first nine months under Sharia, four offenders suffered two-limb amputations, ten more lost their right hands and scores were publicly flogged. In Iran in 1984, a year after Sharia was introduced, over 500 people were flogged and 19 murderers were executed after relatives insisted on the application of the talionic penalty; in a further 51 cases, the relatives accepted blood money.

Nigeria, divided into a mainly Muslim north and Christian and animist south, has a secular legal system, but Sharia courts have long existed in some northern states, confined to civil law and personal status. A strict application of Sharia was introduced in 12 northern states between 2000 and 2002 following demands from the local people. The new laws ban alcohol and sex outside marriage, prevent women working in many jobs and impose sexual segregation in schools. The old punishments of stoning and amputation, scrapped under British rule, have been reinstated.

The impetus behind the reintroduction of Sharia came not from the political leaders but from ordinary Muslims. As the British newspaper, the *Guardian* put it:

> There is little doubt that many ordinary Nigerians embrace Islamic law as an act of desperation rather than a religious value system. Islamic intellectuals may talk of Sharia as a rulebook for life, but it is sold to many ordinary Muslims as a solution after so many failed alternatives – democracy, military rule and now the reign of President Olusegun Obasanjo.

Obasanjo has been implicated in massacres of civilian opponents in 1999 and 2001, among a number of other atrocities. The question of why Obasanjo, a Christian, should permit the introduction of Sharia can be answered purely and simply in terms of the votes of the Muslim half of the population of Nigeria; Sharia is a vote-winner with poor, powerless Muslims. In Nigeria, as with other recent Sharia converts, strict penalties are applied as a show of strength in the battle for law and order. The safeguards and strict evidentiary requirements laid down in Sharia are dispensed with if it will score some political points. As Nadeem Khasmi of the Al-Khoi Foundation of London stated in a BBC (British Broadcasting Corporation) interview, it is debatable whether Sharia is, or has ever been, properly enforced:

> It's really questionable to what extent Sharia as a philosophy is actually applied. One could easily argue that in Pakistan – as in other places – it's applied rather selectively and that certain interpretations are used simply to gain political points on the part of some administrations. It's used willy-nilly; it's used ad hoc. And so there is no systematic Sharia law, in the same way as Saudi Arabia or Iran, where there is a Sharia tradition.

Converts to Sharia have taken to it with zeal but nowhere have the severe *hadd* penalties been consistently applied throughout history. In countries with larger numbers of non-Muslims, practice of Sharia has varied quite considerably. In Malaysia, for example, Muslims are the majority, but the society is cosmopolitan and modern in its outlook and there is no barrier to political involvement in the law. The Kingdom of Jordan was created in 1920 as a secular state and has consistently pursued a moderate stance. 'The Jordan example' is discussed throughout the Arab world as an example of the successful moderation of Islamic views by the power and influence of the state. Islamic groups were banned (as also were Communists) until 1991. Since then both groups have gained significant numbers of seats in Parliament, but Jordan's position has, nevertheless, remained moderate.

CONVERTS TO SHARIA HAVE TAKEN TO IT WITH ZEAL BUT NOWHERE HAVE THE SEVERE *HADD* PENALTIES BEEN CONSISTENTLY APPLIED THROUGHOUT HISTORY.

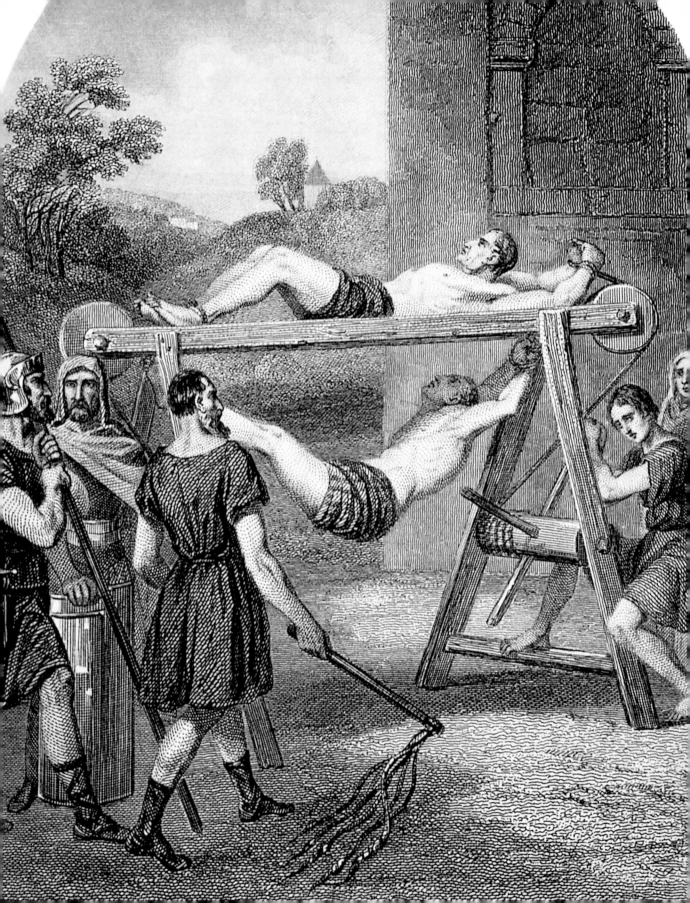

CHAPTER THREE

DEMOCRACY & LAW: THE EUROPEAN LEGACY

I t has been said of the Romans that their greatest legacy was their law. Certainly it has been their most enduring. Long after Rome's temples and aqueducts had crumbled, its law lived on, incorporated into the legal codes of Europe. But as with so many things, the Romans borrowed much of their law from the Greeks, who in this case borrowed it from the Mesopotamians. The Greek Mycaenean civilisation (c. 1400–1200 BCE) incorporated aspects of Babylonian law and Eastern legal ideas continued to travel westward with the trade routes of archaic and classical Greece. Many of the legal rights and procedures enshrined in democratic Athens have their origin in the Code of Hammurabi.

THE ATHENIAN LEGACY

Of all the contributions made to the modern world by Greek civilization, the greatest was undoubtedly democracy, which began in Athens in the eighth century BCE. It was the common people's demands for legal rights that led ultimately to the Athenian democratic experiment. The first moves towards democratic legal rights were made centuries before, in the long dark age that followed the end of the Mycenaean civilization in the 12th century BCE.

During this time, art, culture and writing were lost, the economy collapsed and the population dwindled. In the absence of centralized government, power devolved to local kings. The monarchs' powers were, in theory, total; they had absolute authority over their region, control of religious rites and the power to judge and punish wrongdoers. However, their ability to coerce their followers was limited. As the contemporary Greek poet Hesiod points out,

LEFT: The real or imagined horrors of Roman punishments have fed the imagination for centuries. This 19th-century illustration shows an entirely fanciful Roman rack tightened by a windlass.

ABOVE: The Council of Areopagus, which met periodically to discuss matters of state importance and consider capital cases. It was one of the first representative bodies of Athens.

their authority depended ultimately on the people's consent: 'When his people in their assembly get on the wrong track, he gently sets matters right, persuading them with soft words.'

But the grievances experienced by the lower classes at the hands of the law escalated to such an extent that eventually 'soft words' were no longer enough.

Homer gives us an insight into Dark Age justice in his epic poems the *Iliad* and the *Odyssey*, written in the eighth century BCE but set probably about 400 years earlier. The state punished offenders who threatened society, but as with all personal offences, homicide was considered a private matter. Public trials were held to determine guilt, but prosecution and punishment were the responsibility of the victim's family.

The first purpose of a trial was to see if the victim's family could be persuaded to accept blood money as compensation for the death. If they accepted it, the court recorded the payment and forbade the victim's family from pursuing any further compensation or exacting revenge on the offender.

The old Dark Age values had dictated that it was weak and shameful not to avenge an offence, and blood feuds were common. In the early years of the Athenian *polis*, punishment was still largely a private matter between the perpetrator and the victim, but injured parties had the choice of Homeric arbitration or of bringing the accused to trial. Magistrates were all regional aristocrats, labelled 'bribe-devouring kings' who oppressed the people with their 'crooked decisions' by Hesiod. Those without power or influence had no real access to justice; lower-class citizens were not even allowed to sue in court, but were forced to find an upper-class citizen willing to represent them and speak on their behalf.

During the Dark Age, the most prominent of the king's followers rose in power and influence, so that by the eighth century BCE, Athens was ruled by the *eupatridae*, a class of hereditary aristocrats. Just as the kings depended on aristocratic consent to rule, the aristocrats could not entirely ignore the wishes of the commoners and peasants. The lower classes had some limited rights of representation at aristocratic assemblies and resort to arbitration to settle grievances. One of the earliest Athenian institutions was the Council of Areopagus, an aristocratic body with judicial and legislative powers:

> The Council of Areopagus was guardian of the laws, and kept a watch on the magistrates to make them govern in accordance with the laws. A person unjustly treated might lay a complaint before the Council … stating the law in contravention of which he was treated unjustly.
>
> (Aristotle, *Athenian Constitution*, IV, 4)

By the time the Athenian city-state or *polis* was founded in about 750 BCE, aristocratic power had begun to slip. Social conditions had changed, the economy had recovered and population levels were booming, most rapidly in the peasant class. A new non-aristocratic middle class, made prosperous by agriculture and trade, began to demand political and legal rights and protection from the arbitrary decisions of monarchs.

> But the rule of the multitude has in the first place the loveliest name of all, equality, and does in the second place none of the things that a monarch does. It determines offices by lot, and holds power accountable, and conducts all deliberating publicly. Therefore I give my opinion that we make an end of monarchy and exalt the multitude, for all things are possible for the majority.
>
> (Hesiod, *Histories*, LXXX: 3, 6)

THE AEROPAGUS IN HOMER

Meanwhile the people were gathered in assembly, for there was a quarrel, and two men were wrangling about the blood-price for a man who had died, the one claiming to the district that he had the right to pay off the damages in full, and the other refusing to accept anything. Each was seeking a limit, in the presence of an arbitrator, and the people took sides, each man backing the side that he had taken; but the heralds kept them back, and the elders sat on their seats of stone in a solemn circle, holding the staves which the heralds had put into their hands. Then they rose and each in his turn gave judgment, and there were two measures of gold laid down, to be given to him whose judgment should be deemed the fairest.

(Homer, *Iliad*, XVIII: 497–508)

By the late seventh century BCE, a fledgling democracy was in place. All freeborn adult male citizens of Athens had the right to attend the meetings of a body called the *ekklesia* ('assembly'), which elected nine archons as rulers and magistrates. The aristocrats were still powerful, however, controlling the selection of archons and competing with each other for political power.

Draco's code

In Athens, the poet Hesiod, a lower-class citizen who had himself suffered injustices under the law, agitated for a written code that would protect the rights of all citizens. Hesiod's writing stirred up resentment not just in the middle class but in the poor, who were beginning to realize their collective power, particularly after they rallied 'from the fields in a body' as Hesiod put it, to crush an attempted coup by the aristocrat Cylon in 632 BCE.

These public pressures led in 621 BCE to the appointment of the archon Draco to compile a legal code in the hope of promoting stability and equality. Draco, whose name is the origin of the word 'Draconian', embraced the notion of state punishment rather too enthusiastically. His code mandated the death penalty for virtually all crimes, even minor ones such as petty theft. When asked about the harshness of his punishments, Draco is believed to have said that the death penalty was an appropriate punishment for stealing even so much as a cabbage.

> … One penalty was assigned to almost all transgressions, namely death, so that even those convicted of idleness were put to death, and those who stole salad or fruit received the same punishment as those who committed sacrilege or murder. Therefore Demades, in later times, made a hit when he said that Draco's laws were written not with ink, but blood. And Draco himself, they say, being asked why he made death the penalty for most offences, replied that in his opinion the lesser ones deserved it, and for the greater ones no heavier penalty could be found.
>
> (Plutarch, *Lives*, XVII: 1–2)

Draco's code set down penalties for homicide, though in these he probably followed established customary law; by his time, homicide was probably already punished exclusively by the state. For premeditated murder the penalty was death, but after the opening arguments of the trial had been heard the offender was permitted to flee Athens and exile himself to another Greek state. Exile was the usual punishment for the other two forms of homicide: 'impassioned' (out of anger or love) and involuntary. Killings proved to be in self-defence were not punished.

DRACO EMBRACED THE NOTION OF STATE PUNISHMENT RATHER TOO EAGERLY. HIS CODE MANDATED THE DEATH PENALTY FOR VIRTUALLY ALL CRIMES, EVEN VERY MINOR ONES SUCH AS PETTY THEFT.

Exiles could not attend public games, enter temples or participate in sacrifices. Provided they followed these rules, the state protected the exiles from attack by the victim's family who were under pain of punishment by the Athenian authorities. Any citizen could put exiles that violated their conditions or returned illegally to Athens to death. Murderers remained in exile for life, but other killers could return, with full restoration of citizenship, if the victim's family decided the debt was paid.

The homicide provisions were thus still partly dependent on the victim's family, but from Draco's time onwards the state brought prosecutions for homicide and for other serious crimes. State involvement in homicide trials was influenced by a new attitude that saw killing as 'impure' and potentially contaminating to society, necessitating the death or exile of offenders. Proceedings for unpremeditated homicide started with a public proclamation prohibiting the accused from entering the marketplace and temples, to protect the public from his contamination.

The Draconian code did not silence unrest in Athens; it inflamed it. It was not the code's harsh criminal punishments, however, but its provisions for civil debt that caused the most upheaval and resentment. Under Draco's code, debtors who could not pay were punished by being sold into slavery, either working directly for their creditors or sold to another *polis*. Many debtors escaped slavery by voluntary exile.

Athens suffered a severe economic slump in the years after the introduction of Draco's code, with the result that huge numbers of people were made debt-slaves. Agricultural production was threatened as the land was stripped of peasant farmers, and once-prosperous middle-class citizens found themselves slipping into debt and facing the prospect of losing all they had. The only beneficiaries of this chaos were rich and aristocratic families, who were made richer by the seizure of debtors' land and property. Draco's code set rich squarely against poor, and 25 years after the introduction of his code there was a very real danger of civil war in Athens.

Solon's reforms

In 594 BCE, the merchant, politician and poet Solon was appointed to revise the political, economic and social structure of Athens and issue a new legal code to give greater consideration to the middle-class and poor. Solon's reforms set Athens firmly on the course towards a democratic society.

Solon was entrusted with the responsibility because as a wealthy shipowner and member of a respectable family, he was accepted by the upper classes, and as a commoner engaged in trade he was also accepted by the poor. He successfully arbitrated a compromise, stopping short of revolutionizing

'HOW CAN MONARCHY BE A FIT THING, WHEN THE RULER CAN DO WHAT HE WANTS WITH IMPUNITY? GIVE THIS POWER TO THE BEST MAN ON EARTH, AND IT WOULD STIR HIM TO UNACCUSTOMED THOUGHTS….' (HESIOD, *HISTORIES*, LXXX: 3, 6)

RIGHT: The philosopher
Aristotle was banished
from Athens. Here, he
leaves with his followers,
having been falsely accused
of impiety.

society, but ensuring the participation of many more citizens in the political
process. Solon reformed only what he thought the Athenians would accept;
when later asked whether he had made the best laws he could for the
Athenians, Solon replied: 'The best they were able to receive.'

Solon ended the practice of creditors legally enslaving their debtors. Those
who had become slaves were freed, and those who had been sold to foreigners
or had fled abroad returned to Athens as free men. Outstanding debts were
cancelled and seized property was returned. Solon retained Draco's statutes
only in relation to murder and treason, abolishing the death penalty for all
other crimes.

Neither rich nor poor got all they wanted from Solon's reforms. There was
no universal redistribution of wealth as demanded by the poor, and the rich
grumbled at losing the money owed to them. But the reforms had a generally
beneficial effect on the peace and stability of Athenian society and allowed for
participation of many more citizens in the political process.

Solon, in addition to his other skills, was an accomplished poet, and in this
fragment of a poem he sums up his deeds as a lawgiver:

And many Athenians sold into slavery – some justly, some not – did I bring
home to their god-founded land, while others, having fled their debts under

Necessity's compulsion, no longer spoke the Attic tongue (since they wandered to all parts of the earth), and others here, bound in shameful servitude and trembling before the harsh character of their masters, I set free. I achieved these things, forcefully yoking force and justice together, and I proceeded on the course that I had promised. I composed ordinances for base and noble alike, fitting straight justice for each.

LEFT: Solon the Lawgiver. Solon's reforms of 594 BCE abolished the harsh punishments of Draco's code and made better provision for the middle-class and poor. Civil unrest, which had threatened to break out under Draco, was averted.

LAW IN THE ROMAN REPUBLIC AND EMPIRE

While democracy may be Greece's outstanding contribution to the modern world, law can be counted as perhaps the most enduring of Rome's many historical legacies. The Roman era started with a legal code, the Twelve Tables, and ended, almost 1000 years later, with a new one, the Code of Justinian. When Justinian compiled his Code, he claimed to have condensed a million words into 5000, and his neat encapsulation of 1000 years of evolving Roman law served – although he wasn't to know it – as a kind of time capsule, a legacy that would survive the fall of the Roman Empire to enter the legal codes of Europe.

Rome was first settled at the end of the Bronze Age in about 1000 BCE when farmers gathered their homes together at the lowest crossing-point of the river Tiber. The settlement began to grow into a town controlled by three tribes, each of which was divided into clans and families. Social and political life was dominated by a system of clientship (*clientela*), in which the richer families took responsibility for the poorer ones, demanding a bond of loyalty from them in return.

The dominance of the clan and family in early Roman civil life extended to their concepts of law. *Parricidium*, the murder of a free man, was at first considered a civil, not a criminal, matter, and was punished by members of the victim's family. Other offences against persons, such as theft and corporal injuries, also came under the jurisdiction of civil, not criminal, courts. Religious offences, however, were considered an offence against divine order and so were punished by the state. Vestal virgins who broke their vows, for example, were punished by death.

Punishment of those who broke the law was seen as a necessary religious expiation that would restore essential divine order. In early Roman society, religious expiation and personal revenge remained the main motivations for punishments.

The Republic

The region was ruled by a series of Etruscan kings, but there was also an Assembly, with probably about 300 elected members drawn from the 1000 or so wealthiest families (the patricians.) In about 510 BCE the patricians, with the help of the mass of the Roman population (the plebeians), ousted the last king, Tarquinius Superbus (Tarquin the Proud), and instigated the Republic.

Almost as soon as the Republic was proclaimed, the plebeians challenged the patricians for power, and gradually began to win rights and representation. By the fourth century BCE, tribunes, plebeian magistrates who ran the representative Plebeian Council had been put in place. Despite these

'THE GREATEST ACHIEVEMENT OF THE ROMANS, WHETHER WE CONSIDER IT ON ITS OWN MERITS OR IN ITS INFLUENCE ON THE HISTORY OF THE WORLD, IS WITHOUT DOUBT, THEIR LAW … WHEREAS THE POPULATION OF THE ROMAN EMPIRE MAY HAVE BEEN 50 MILLIONS, AT PRESENT, 870 MILLION PEOPLE LIVE UNDER SYSTEMS TRACEABLE TO ROMAN LAW.'
(R.H. BARROW, *THE ROMANS*)

democratic advances, the clientship system ensured that positions of power were still held by patricians.

The plebeians' demands for equality under the law and protection from the whims of patrician magistrates led to the drawing up of the first Roman legal code, the Twelve Tables, between 451–450 BCE.

The plebeians' growing demands led to the appointment in 455 BCE of a commission of 10 men (*Decemviri*) to draw up a legal code that would be binding on both parties and would ensure the impartiality of magistrates.

After five years, the commission produced ten tables' worth of statutes, some undoubtedly new but most reflecting the state of existing customary laws. The plebeians were not satisfied with this and a second *Decemviri* was appointed, which produced two additional tables.

BELOW: Rome's first legal code, the Twelve Tables is placed in the Forum in 450 BCE. It came about as a direct result of pressure from the common people, the plebeians, who were previously subject to the whims of aristocratic patrician magistrates.

ABOVE: Rome, 485 BCE: Cassius, convicted of political wrongdoing, is thrown to his death from the Tarpeian Rock in Rome. This fate was reserved for those who committed treason or other crimes against the state.

The Twelve Tables

The placing of the laws of the Twelve Tables on public display in the Forum represented a victory for the political and judicial rights of the plebeians. The original bronze tablets were probably destroyed when the Gauls sacked Rome in 387 BCE, but the majority of the Tables are preserved in surviving writings. Although some of the provisions became outdated and were replaced by later laws and legal codes, the Twelve Tables were never abolished and were considered the foundation of Roman law by later legislators in the Republic and Empire.

The aim of the Twelve Tables was to ensure the rights of the average citizen; it was not intended to be a complete legal code. Although it does include criminal law, the main topics covered are the family, marriage and divorce, property, debt and legal procedure. Like a large number of ancient legal codes, the Twelve Tables are written in plain style and each provision conforms to a set pattern – an injunction, a conditional clause or sentence and an imperative imposition:

> Let them keep the road in order. If they have not paved it, a man may drive his team where he likes.

The language has little of the complexity of a modern code that can sometimes lead to confusion:

> If he [the plaintiff] summons to court, he [the defendant] is to go. If he does not go, he [the plaintiff] is to call [someone else] to bear witness. Then he [the plaintiff] is to seize him [the defendant].

The Twelve Tables mark a transitional stage between private revenge and state punishment. The latter is generally reserved for offences against religion and civil security. Such offences would have included not only treason, but also employing malign influence or black magic. The Twelve Tables stipulates the death penalty, for example, for saying a malicious incantation against another person or for performing an exorcism to make another's crops sterile.

Personal assault, up to and including murder, was still a private matter, and the law existed merely to ensure that reparation was made to the injured party, either through monetary recompense or, if agreement could not be reached, a *talio* – retaliation in kind, a state-sponsored private revenge:

> If a person has maimed another's limb, let there be retaliation in kind unless he makes agreement for composition with him.

> If he has broken or bruised a freeman's bone with his hand or a club, he shall undergo a penalty of 300 pieces; if a slave's, 150.

> (VIII, 2–3)

The continued existence of private revenge is demonstrated most forcefully in the provisions on robbery. The victim of a robbery could lawfully kill the robber if he was caught red-handed at night, or even by day if he was armed or resisted arrest. The only proviso was that the victim had to inform his neighbours so they could act as witnesses. Alternatively, the victim could bring the robber before a magistrate, and if the robber was found guilty, the victim had the right to kill him, keep him as a slave or sell him into slavery, or demand a ransom. If the robber was not caught red-handed, the victim had no right to private revenge.

> 'THOUGH ALL THE WORLD EXCLAIM AGAINST ME, I WILL SAY WHAT I THINK: THAT SINGLE LITTLE BOOK OF THE TWELVE TABLES, IF ANYONE LOOK TO THE FOUNTAINS AND SOURCES OF LAWS, SEEMS TO ME, ASSUREDLY, TO SURPASS THE LIBRARIES OF ALL THE PHILOSOPHERS, BOTH IN WEIGHT OF AUTHORITY, AND IN PLENITUDE OF UTILITY. (CICERO, *DE ORATORE*, I: 44)

The Twelve Tables mandated the death penalty for a number of crimes, including theft by night in the city and treason.

Just as in the Babylonian code, arson was punishable by burning:

Any person who destroys by burning any building or heap of corn deposited alongside a house shall be bound, scourged, and put to death by burning at the stake provided that he has committed the said misdeed with malice aforethought; but if he shall have committed it by accident, that is, by negligence, it is ordained that he repair the damage or, if he be too poor to be competent for such punishment, he shall receive a lighter punishment.

(VIII, 10)

According to the Tables, debtors could be punished by being sold into slavery, but had to be sold abroad, implying that Roman citizens could not act as slaves in Rome. There was also a lesser punishment of *nexum* (temporary bondage) for non-payment of debt. The victim remained a citizen and could end his punishment by repaying the debt.

One who has confessed a debt, or against whom judgment has been pronounced, shall have 30 days to pay it in. After that forcible seizure of his person is allowed. The creditor shall bring him before the magistrate. Unless he pays the amount of the judgment or some one in the presence of the magistrate interferes in his behalf as protector the creditor so shall take him home and fasten him in stocks or fetters. He shall fasten him with not less than 15 pounds of weight or, if he choose, with more. If the prisoner choose, he may furnish his own food. If he does not, the creditor must give him a pound of meal daily; if he choose he may give him more.

(III, 1)

The Twelve Tables set out trial procedure that was followed throughout the years of the Republic and Empire, and established legal rights that have been incorporated into the modern legal systems of countries around the world.

The code's first provision, for example, states that it is compulsory for witnesses to attend trial when summoned. A later provision calls for honesty and impartiality among judges, and stipulates the death penalty for judges found guilty of accepting bribes. The code also explicitly states the need for evidence before conviction:

Putting to death of any man, whosoever he might be unconvicted is forbidden.

(IX, 6)

The code also makes provision for changes to the law by popular consent, enshrining the principle that the law is the servant of the people:

Whatever the people had last ordained should be held as binding by law.

(XII, 5)

While such stipulations are still in use today, some of the provisions in the Twelve Tables rapidly became obsolete in their own era. When the Tables were first drawn up, Rome was still a small and semi-rural settlement. As Rome grew, so did its crime rate, and it became clear that the Twelve Tables' scant criminal law provisions were inadequate and its reliance on private vengeance unworkable for such a large and complex society. Gradually, the state began to take over as the instrument of punishment.

In the third century BCE, a police force was introduced, with judicial powers to deal harshly with dangerous miscreants including delinquents, thieves, arsonists and poisoners. The death penalty was the answer for most of these crimes. Mere possession of poison was a capital crime, as was carrying arms with criminal intent.

In the second century BCE, a permanent court system began to develop. Previously, a commission that had been specially convened for the occasion would have dealt with serious crimes. In 122 BCE, Gaius Gracchus introduced the *Lex Sempronia Iudiciaria*, a law that established permanent tribunals for serious offences and specified that they did not have to be composed of

ABOVE: Rome, 64 CE: the Emperor Nero orders the upside-down crucifixion of the Apostle Peter. Nero blamed the Christians for the Great Fire that devastated the city of Rome and had hundreds of Christians executed.

senators. This law democratized the court system and brought about the system of trial by jury that was the mainstay of criminal justice in the late Republic and Empire. But that did not necessarily mean that jury trials were any fairer. In cases involving alleged crimes against the state, juries were often packed to ensure a guilty verdict against troublesome political opponents.

In the late Republic and particularly in the Empire, earlier Republican laws were extended and generally harsher penalties were applied. Offences that had

JUSTINIAN'S DIGEST

Law is the act of the good and the fair ... Justice is the constant and perpetual will to give each man his right.
(Justinian, *Digest*)

In 324 CE, the emperor Constantine made Christianity the official state religion, and in 330 he moved his capital to Byzantium, renaming it Constantinopolis (Constantinople). The Empire was split into two parts, a western empire based in Rome and an eastern empire based in Constantinople. While the eastern empire thrived, surviving until 1453, Rome was invaded by waves of barbarians, before falling in 476 with the overthrow of the last emperor, Romulus Augustulus.

As the Roman Empire was coming to an end, the Byzantine emperor Justinian (483 CE–565 CE) came to the throne. Justinian is known for two great achievements, the construction of the St Sophia cathedral in Constantinople and the compilation in 529 CE of the *Corpus Juris Civilis*, ('Body of Civil Law'), also called the *Codex Justinianus* or Code of Justinian.

Justinian's legal code included the Digest (*Digesta*), a clear and concise distillation of 1000 years of Roman imperial law that served as a direct model for the laws of much of Europe. Roman law was established in the lands of the Holy Roman Empire, and was applied in Germany right up to the end of the 19th century where it did not conflict with local legislation until 1900. The *Codex Justinianus* was the model for the French Code Napolon, and the perceived clarity and logic of Roman legal codes was a major influence on the codification movement of the 19th century that gave birth to the civil codes of Germany, Switzerland and Austria.

Many of the provisions of the *Codex Justinianus* have become basic tenets of modern law, such as 'The burden of proof is upon the party affirming, not the party denying' and 'A father is not a competent witness for a son, nor a son for a father.'

previously been considered private (*delicta*) began to be considered public penal matters (*crimina*). During the reign of the first emperor, Augustus (63 BCE–14 CE), new criminal offences included adultery with an honourable lady, organizing a criminal gang and beating or killing a citizen without provocation.

Augustus introduced another important innovation, the establishment of an effective police force. He appointed a senator to the post of prefect of the city (*praefectus urbi*) and placed at his disposal a strengthened and improved police force, which was effective in combating delinquency and banditry in the city. Police courts were reorganized and placed under the jurisdiction of the *praefectus urbi*. These courts were so efficient at processing cases and punishing crimes that they began to replace jury trials.

Augustus is remembered as a wise and just ruler, but the same could not be said for a surprising number of his successors. In the reign of the demented Nero or the bloodthirsty Domitian, the written law took second place to the brutal whim of the emperor. However, in long periods of stability and just rule, those who accepted and were ruled by Roman law benefited from the protection it offered. Roman law is the origin of modern legal concepts, such as natural rights or equality before the law, even if in Rome such concepts were often honoured more in the breach than the observance.

Roman punishments

The main punishments in the Republic and Empire were execution, exile, corporal punishment, imprisonment and fines.

The ultimate sanction (*summum supplicium*) of the death penalty was very rarely applied to Roman citizens, or at least, high-ranking ones. For slaves, foreigners and even low-ranking citizens there were many capital crimes. Arson, for example, was usually punished by banishment, but arson for plunder in a city could earn a death sentence.

Methods of execution included burning, stoning, crucifixion, the *furca* (hanging from a large fork until dead) and being thrown to the animals. Burning was reserved for slaves and *humiliores* (low-ranking freeman). It was used primarily for plotting against your masters, occasionally for sacrilege, and for deserters and magicians. After the Great Fire of Rome in 64 CE, the emperor Nero regularly burned Christians, who he decided to blame for starting the fire. When Vespasian put down a Jewish revolt in Cyrene, in present-day Libya, he tortured its leader, Jonathan and then burned him alive.

Crucifixion was the standard method of execution for slaves and low-ranking foreigners. The law did not forbid the crucifixion of citizens, but

> IN THE REIGN OF THE DEMENTED NERO OR THE BLOODTHIRSTY DOMITIAN, THE WRITTEN LAW TOOK SECOND PLACE TO THE BRUTAL WHIM OF THE EMPEROR.

instances are extremely rare and unusual enough to excite comment. When Galba, the governor of Baetica, crucified a Roman citizen, contemporary historian Suetonius described the act as 'excessively cruel'. The victim was reported to have 'implored the laws' and 'testified to his Roman citizenship' during his trial.

When Nero wasn't burning Christians he was crucifying them, a practice that continued after the emperor's death. Nero is also recorded as punishing a group of Jewish rebels arrested in Jerusalem with scourging and crucifixion. Crucifixion was later banned by Constantine and replaced by the simple but highly effective *furca*. The victim was to hang by the neck from a fork until dead.

Being thrown to the animals was a punishment reserved for slaves, foreigners and free men guilty of very serious offences, which included sacrilege. Considered a 'light' form of capital punishment, it was sometimes applied to citizens; Claudius is known to have thrown a number of citizens to the beasts.

Corporal punishment was used against slaves and foreigners. Criminals were also branded, often on the face, until the practice was banned by Constantine in 315 CE.

Torture was not permitted for high ranks (*honestiores*), but that certainly did not stop it happening. Those guilty of treason, of whatever rank, were regularly tortured, as of course was anyone who had displeased the Emperor.

Claudius started his reign with an oath not to use torture, but in the second year of his reign, he crushed the revolt of Camillus Scribonianus and tortured all the rebels, including high-born foreigners and citizens. In Tiberius's most excessive period, he used torture freely against free men and citizens. According to Suetonius, Gaius treated his dinner guests to displays of conspirators being tortured.

Torture was also used judicially against slaves. In fact, the evidence of slaves could only be legally admitted under torture, which was carried out in court. The practice of judicial torture later endured in the ecclesiastical courts of medieval Europe.

During most of the Republic, high-ranking citizens escaped capital punishment by opting for the voluntary, convenient and honourable option of exile. By the end of the Republic, however, exile was made a legal penalty. Anyone who was exiled would normally also be stripped of his citizenship and have his assets seized, but in some cases a less severe form of exile was imposed. Higher ranks could be given *libera custodia* (free custody), which meant being confined to an Italian town but retaining full rights of citizenship. Ulpian described the options available in *De officio proconsulis*:

BEING THROWN TO THE ANIMALS WAS A PUNISHMENT RESERVED FOR SLAVES, FOREIGNERS AND FREE MEN GUILTY OF VERY SERIOUS OFFENCES, WHICH INCLUDED SACRILEGE.

Concerning the custody of accused men, the proconsul is accustomed to decide whether in each case the person should be put in prison, or handed over to a soldier, or entrusted to guarantors, or even to himself. He usually makes this decision in accordance with the kind of crime, which is charged, or the standing of the person accused, or his great wealth, or his innocence, or his dignity.

ABOVE: The public spectacles of imperial Rome attracted huge crowds. Death by wild animals is a fate associated with early Christians, but it was applied equally to Jews and, at times, even to the Emperor's enemies.

Fines were levied for lesser offences. The Twelve Tables sets out fines to be levied for assault and slander:

If one has maimed a limb and does not compromise with the injured person, let there be retaliation. If one has broken a bone of a freeman with his hand or with a cudgel, let him pay a penalty of three hundred coins. If he has broken the bone of a slave, let him have one hundred and fifty coins. If one is guilty of insult, the penalty shall be twenty-five coins.'

(VIII, 2)

CHAPTER FOUR

INDIA AND CHINA

The legal traditions of India and China both developed independently of the European and Middle Eastern laws derived from those of Mesopotamia. The primary documents are the Indian Laws of Manu, compiled in the first or second century CE, and the Chinese Tang Code, written in the eighth century. The Laws of Manu were never universally applied all over India and represented an idealised picture of society from the point of view of the ruling Brahman caste. The Tang Code, however, was the law of the land throughout a vast empire and was a blueprint for the imperial codes of the next millennium. In each case, the laws were enforced by a network of police, magistrates and informers, and in the case of Tang China, by a vast empire-wide civil service.

INDIA

India's history is inextricably bound up with the history of Hinduism, which existed long before the writing of the first Hindu sacred and instructional texts, the *Vedas*, between 1500 and 500 BCE. The writers of the *Vedas*, the Aryans, are thought to have originated from Persia and to have invaded India shortly before 2000 BCE, first settling in Punjab and Sind, although some recent scholars believe they were, in fact, indigenous to India. Over the following centuries, they created the social and spiritual foundations of India, which endure, in many respects, to this day. The Aryans brought with them a system of social segregation that divided society into four classes. Each class had its own rules and position within society, but there was very limited movement between the classes. As Hinduism developed and spread, this class segregation hardened into the strict caste system that still pervades modern Indian society.

During the Vedic age, the system of segregation was known as *varga* ('colour') and was afterwards known as *jati* ('birth'). In the sixteenth century, Portuguese travellers to India encountered this system and described it by using the Portuguese word for clan or family, *casta*.

LEFT: These two Chinese highwaymen from about 1900 are punished with the *cangue*, a hinged board worn around the neck. Like the pillory and stocks in Europe, the cangue is uncomfortable, but the real punishment is public humiliation or bodily injury at the hands of onlookers.

The basic four castes are the *kshatriyas*, *brahmans*, *vaishyas* and *shudras*. Top of the heap are the *kshatriyas*, who, according to a Vedic hymn, sprung from the arms of the gods. Within this caste were kings, nobles and soldiers. The next caste was made up of the *brahmans* or priests, said to be born from the mouth of the gods. The brahmans grew in power and importance until they came to dominate Indian society from 600 to 200 BCE, a period now known as the Brahmanic Age. Below them were the *vaishyas* who were defined as being born of the thighs of the gods and included the merchants, farmers, traders and other freemen. The lowest caste was the *shudras* or serfs, said to be born of the feet of the gods. This class was referred to as the 'untouchables' by the higher castes and its members were treated as barely human.

The system was designed to maintain the racial purity of the Aryan noble and *brahman* castes. So afraid of contamination were they that they listed over 40 categories of 'impure' human beings descended from the various primitive tribes who had settled in India. Among the lowest of the low were the *chandala* or pariahs (from the Tamil word *paraiyan*, meaning 'low caste'). The pariahs could not leave their isolated rural villages without striking a wooden clapper to warn of their approach. The touch, breath, or even sight of a pariah was believed to be so impure that it would contaminate the other castes.

In a society as strictly divided as this, it was inevitable that a defendant's treatment at the hands of the law would be inextricably bound up with the hapless circumstance of his or her birth.

BELOW: An Indian funeral procession of 1820, from the book *Lives of the Brahmins*, showing the body of an old *brahman* carried on a stretcher and attended by mourners. Since the days of the Laws of Manu, *brahmans* have guarded their position of influence and power in Indian society.

Dharma is rendered in English as 'law', but the Indian concept of *dharma* is closer to a divine moral code that determines the right path to take in life. Each person has his own *dharma*, adapted to his abilities, his role in life and, above all, his caste. Punishment was a necessary religious expiation for the criminal. If a crime went unpunished, it contaminated the criminal's *karma* so that he would not be favourably reincarnated in the next life.

Conveniently for the dominant *brahmans*, this philosophy provides a divine justification for the exercise of state power by force (*danda*):

> Danda protects all subjects. When they are sleeping, danda keeps awake. Law is nothing but danda itself.
>
> *(Laws of Manu, VIII, 14)*

The Laws of Manu

The Laws of Manu is the common English term for the *Manava Dharma-sastra*, a compendium in Sanskrit verse of ancient laws and customs. Its reputed author is Manu, the mythical survivor of the flood, father of the human race and teacher of sacred rites and law. The introduction describes how the ten great ancient sages approached Manu and asked him to declare to them the sacred laws of the castes; he did by dictating them to the sage Bhrigu.

Despite this claim, the work is believed to have been written in the first or second century CE, although much of its contents had undoubtedly been transmitted orally for centuries. Most scholars believe that the Laws of Manu are, at least in part, a reworking of the lost text *Manava Dharma-sutra*, dating from approximately 500 BCE.

Sutras were manuals of instruction composed by religious teachers for their students. The *sutras* expounded the correct rules, laws, customs and rites for every aspect of life. For example, the *Grihya-sutras* dealt with domestic ceremonies, and the *Dharma-sutras* dealt with sacred customs and laws. From time to time some of the more popular *Dharma-sutras* were compiled, added to and recast in verse in a *Dharma-sastra*, of which the Laws of Manu is one.

A manual of religious, civil and moral instruction written entirely from the *brahmans*' point of view, the Laws of Manu is largely concerned with enumerating the rights and responsibilities of the *brahmans*, with only about a third directly relating to crimes and punishments. However, in one case, that of robbery, the crime was considered so shameful and unworthy of the high-born that the normal order was reversed and punishments were stricter for *brahmans* than for other castes. A *brahman* found guilty of robbery was fined 64 times the value of the property, a *kshatrya* was fined 32 times, a *vaishya* 16 times, and a *shudra* only eight times.

MEN WHO HAVE COMMITTED CRIMES AND HAVE BEEN PUNISHED BY THE KING GO TO HEAVEN, BEING PURE LIKE THOSE WHO ARE IN THE RIGHT TRACK. (LAWS OF MANU, VIII, 318)

> **A SCALE OF PUNISHMENT**
>
> Each caste had its own scale of punishments. Harsh punishments rained down on the lower castes for a wide variety of crimes, while *brahmans* were fined or escaped punishment altogether. *Brahmans* were exempt from the death penalty, receiving no stronger punishment than exile, even for murder. *Shudras*, on the other hand, were subject to corporal punishment for even the most minor crimes.
>
> *Manu, the son of the Self-existent, has named ten places on which punishment may be made to fall in the cases of the three lower castes; but a Brahman shall depart unhurt [from the country].*
>
> *These are the organ, the belly, the tongue, the two hands, and fifthly the two feet, the eye, the nose, the two ears, likewise the whole body.*
>
> (VIII, 124–125)
>
> Murder of a *brahman* was a capital offence, and assault or defamation of a *brahman* by a member of a lower caste was dealt with by sympathetic corporal punishment:
>
> *With whatever limb a man of a low caste does hurt to a man of the three highest castes, even that limb shall be cut off; that is the teaching of Manu.*
>
> *…If out of arrogance he spits on a superior, the king shall cause both his lips to be cut off; if he urinates on him, the penis; if he breaks wind against him, the anus.*
>
> (VIII, 279–280, 282–283)
>
> Defamation of members of the higher castes by a *shudra* was treated equally harshly:
>
> *A once-born man [a shudra], who insults a twice-born man with gross invective, shall have his tongue cut out; for he is of low origin.*
>
> *If he mentions the names and castes of the twice-born with contumely [insulting language], an iron nail, ten fingers long, shall be thrust red-hot into his mouth.*
>
> (VIII, 270–272)

'HE WHO RAISES HIS HAND OR A STICK, SHALL HAVE HIS HAND CUT OFF; HE WHO IN ANGER KICKS WITH HIS FOOT, SHALL HAVE HIS FOOT CUT OFF.'
(LAWS OF MANU)

Evidence and trials

Since punishment of a crime was essential for a soul's passage through life and afterlife, it was crucially important to make sure that justice was properly done. Evidence was collected and assembled and witnesses were called to testify, with an obligation to tell the truth under oath or to incur severe penalties for perjury if they did not. Witnesses to homicides were required to give evidence in court.

In cases where there were no witnesses, trial by ordeal was used to determine guilt, and the Laws of Manu provides an impressive array of methods. Similar to trial by hot water in medieval Europe, there was trial by cow-dung. A pot of cow-dung mixed with oil was heated to boiling point and the accused was made to bury his arm in it. If he escaped being burned, he was innocent. In trial by poison, the accused was blindfolded and made to retrieve a ring from a basket containing a poisonous snake. In trial by fire, he had to walk through fire or carry a hot iron ball.

There was also trial by *dharma* and *adharma*. Symbols of justice (*dharma*) and injustice (*adharma*) were drawn onto leaves painted white and black respectively. The leaves were then rolled into balls, immersed in mud to conceal them and placed in a jar. The accused was asked to pick a ball. If he picked *dharma* he was innocent, but if he picked *adharma* he was pronounced guilty.

The courts were supported by a police force with officers stationed in most villages. The officers not only kept order but also investigated crimes and amassed evidence to bring to trial. There was also a system of paid informers and volunteers, whose main task was to seek out official corruption and popular rebellion, as well as petty crime. These government spies were secreted in the villages posing as scholars, priests or ascetics, or else were recruited from sectors of society normally avoided by Hindus, such as dwarfs, mutes, hunchbacks and transsexuals. The spies were fully authorized to act as agents provocateurs, by, for example, bribing a judge to give a favourable verdict in a trial was a regular practice. Entrapment of corrupt officials was considered a perfectly legal and honourable means of rooting out and punishing those who abused their position.

Application of the laws

To a large extent, the Laws of Manu represents the *brahmans'* ideal picture of what the laws ought to be. But in practice, not all of the statutes would have been applied at all times. India's vast territory meant that laws would have been difficult to impose uniformly, and local kings and princes could dispense justice as they pleased. Judges also often administered gentler punishments than

BELOW: This illustration depicts the god Vishnu, preserver of the universe and one of the holy trinity of the Supreme God. It is taken from an edition of the earliest Hindu sacred text, the *Rig Veda*, probably compiled in about 1500 BCE. The writers of *Rig Veda*, the Aryans from Persia, laid the social and religious foundations of India by promoting the caste system that persists to this day. The Laws of Manu used religious beliefs to justify the authority of the upper caste, the *brahmans*.

those prescribed. Mindful of their responsibility to avoid punishing the innocent, they erred on the side of leniency. The circumstances of the crime and the social standing, mental state, age or health of the criminal were all mitigating factors.

Many of the more gruesome corporal punishments were only carried out on repeat offenders when it was considered that gentler punishments had had no effect. The Laws of Manu prescribes a warning for a first offender, a heavy fine for a third-time offender and mutilation of the body only for an incorrigible recidivist.

> Let him punish first by admonition, afterwards by reproof, thirdly by a fine, after that by corporal chastisement.
>
> (VIII, 129)

THE LAW OF THE TANG DYNASTY

North China has been inhabited from at least the time of Peking Man, some 500,000 years ago. Although it is impossible to prove that Peking Man is a direct ancestor of the modern Chinese, it seems the pure 'Han' Chinese from North China have simply always been there. Certainly, by about 10,000 BCE,

Neolithic settlements were established across China, and by about 1500 BCE writing, bronze making and a national bureaucracy had all been established under the Shang, the first verifiable Chinese dynasty.

For many years China developed in isolation, protected by natural borders on three sides and the Great Wall on the other. Built to keep out invaders from the north, the Great Wall was begun in the third century BCE and was extended in fits and starts over several centuries. These borders, both natural and man-made, meant that China's legal system developed entirely independently of the Middle Eastern and European codes, which claim a common root in Mesopotamian law.

The first Chinese legal code referred to by name is the *Fa Jing* (Canon of Laws), compiled in the fourth century BCE and based on previous legal codes dating back at least three centuries. According to later texts, the Canon of Laws dealt with theft, robbery, arrest, prison and judicial rules, and enumerated five permitted corporal punishments: tattooing of the forehead or face, cutting off the nose, amputation of one or both feet, castration and death.

The Canon of Laws served as a model for the legal code developed by the Legalist government of the Qin dynasty (221–207 BCE). The Legalists believed that the sole unifying factor in society was the force of the state as expressed through law. With the goal of unifying China's great territory in mind, they introduced the first written laws, minutely categorizing a huge array of offences carrying numerous and fierce penalties. Their efforts were met with success – but at a terrible social cost. Force alone was not enough to keep China united for long and the dynasty ended in 206 BCE after only 25 years. Despite their short-lived reign, the Qin's legal code was adopted as a starting point for legal codes of later dynasties. Each code was a revision of the previous one, synthesizing the legal and philosophical beliefs of the past with the thought and practice of the present.

The next benchmark in China's legal history was established 800 years later, during a golden age of the Tang empire.

'PUNISHMENT SHOULD BE ACCORDED TO THE MERITS OF EACH CASE, AFTER DUE CONSIDERATION OF THE MIND OF THE OFFENDER AND THE CIRCUMSTANCES UNDER WHICH THE OFFENCE WAS COMMITTED.' (LAWS OF MANU, VIII, 126)

The Tang Code

Under the Tang dynasty (618–907 CE), China became the largest, richest and most populous empire on earth, extending to Iran, Tibet, Manchuria and most of the Korean peninsula. The Tang capital, Changan (modern Xian), meaning 'eternal peace', was the greatest city in East Asia, with over two million inhabitants and crowds of foreigners come to seek their fortunes.

In this vigorous and cosmopolitan society, the arts flourished. The poetry of Li Bo, fine paintings and ceramics and the first examples of porcelain all date from this period. In 868, Buddhist monks printed the *Diamond Sutra*, the oldest dated printed book in the world. Printing is believed to have existed at least 100 years before this date, based predominantly in Sichuan province.

Last but not least of the Tang dynasty's historical legacy is the creation of a solid and efficient administration, some of whose institutions have survived throughout the imperial era and even to the present day. Staff for the huge Tang bureaucratic and legal system were recruited in part by open examinations, a practice that had first started under the Han but was greatly extended in the Tang era. Under this system, any Chinese citizen – even one of relatively humble birth – had the opportunity to demonstrate his aptitude in an open examination to compete for government jobs.

The Tang Code is the earliest complete Chinese legal code to have survived. Many ancient legal codes claim divine origin for their laws, but the Tang Code states that laws are man-made and created out of necessity. This bald Legalist belief in force is tempered by the Code's frequent appeals to Confucianism as a moral justification. Confucius (Latinised adaptation of *Kong Fuzi*, 551–479 BCE), stated that a stable and orderly society depends on every individual knowing his place in the social and family hierarchy and acting accordingly.

The hierarchy of imperial China is written into the statutes of the Tang Code. Punishments for the same offence varied widely according to the offender's status. Slaves who assaulted a commoner so as to break a limb or put out an eye were executed, while a master who killed a slave without cause received no more than a year of penal servitude. Nobles, relatives of the Emperor and other privileged groups were exempt from most punishments.

For the rest of society, there was a finely graded scale of punishments according to the offender's and the and victim's status. If a high-ranking state official assaulted a junior official two ranks below him, his punishment was reduced by two degrees. If the junior officer assaulted his senior, his punishment was increased by two degrees. Each offence was finely balanced by exactly the right punishment; crime was seen as a disruption of the balance of society, and punishment as a means of restoring it.

The Code is divided into two parts: the first section expounds the general principles of criminal law and the second part enumerates the offences covered, with corresponding punishments for each one. Most statutes are also accompanied by commentaries explaining the offence and justifying the punishment. The Code's 502 articles attempted to list every possible crime and punishment and predict every set of circumstances. This meticulous approach ensured that the administration of justice was automatic and that punishments were uniform throughout the empire. Penalties varied both by type and by degree, depending not only on the nature of the crime but also on the relationship between criminal and victim.

IN ANCIENT CHINA, WOMEN WHO STEPPED OUT OF LINE RECEIVED LIGHTER SENTENCES THAN MEN; THEY WERE BEATEN LESS SEVERELY AND ESCAPED DEATH IN COLLECTIVE PROSECUTIONS, SUFFERING LIFE EXILE OR ENSLAVEMENT INSTEAD. SPECIAL DISPENSATION WAS ALSO GIVEN TO PREGNANT WOMEN. THEY COULD NOT BE BEATEN OR TORTURED, AND A DEATH SENTENCE COULD NOT BE CARRIED OUT ON A PREGNANT WOMAN UNTIL 100 DAYS AFTER THE BABY'S BIRTH.

Article 1 lists five punishments, stating that they were devised by the ancient sages as a reflection of the five elements. Each of the first three punishments is subdivided into five, and there are a total of five subcategories for the last two.

The Five Punishments

1. Light stick: 10, 20, 30, 40 or 50 blows
2. Heavy stick: 60, 70, 80, 90 or 100 blows
3. Penal servitude: 1, 1½, 2, 2½ or 3 years
4. Life exile: 2,000, 2,500 or 3,000 li
   (1 li is about 0.5 km/⅓ mile)
5. Death: strangulation or decapitation

The Ten Abominations

Though the Code attempts to set down every conceivable offence and punishment, some acts were considered so heinous that they were also listed under Article 6, entitled 'The Ten Abominations'.

1 Plotting rebellion	6 Great irreverence
2 Plotting great sedition	7 Lack of filial piety
3 Plotting treason	8 Discord
4 Contumacy	9 Unrighteousness
5 Depravity	10 Incest

ABOVE: Confucius (551–479 BCE) stated that a stable and orderly society depends on every individual knowing his place in the social hierarchy. The Tang Code conveniently borrowed Confucian beliefs to justify the rule of the Emperor, though Confucius believed that positive social influences ought to make written laws unnecessary.

Broadly speaking, these crimes were those that endangered the emperor or the state, those committed by inferiors against their superiors, those that threatened the family and those involving black magic. In cases concerning the Ten Abominations, the special dispensations normally given to certain privileged groups defined in the Code, including relatives of the emperor, nobles, those of high achievement and ability and those deemed 'morally worthy' were not applicable. Cases had to be prosecuted according to the letter of the law. The most serious crimes were the first three (plotting rebellion, plotting great sedition and plotting treason), as they directly affected the safety of the emperor and the state.

The king occupies the most honourable position and receives heaven's precious decrees. Like heaven and earth, he acts to shelter and support, thus

ABOVE: A man on his knees about to be beheaded in front of a crowd during the Boxer Rebellion of 1900. Beheading and strangulation were the only permitted methods of execution under the Tang Code, and beheadings continued to be carried out throughout the imperial period. In the post-imperial era the preferred method has been shooting.

serving as the father and the mother of the masses. As his children, as his subjects, they must be loyal and filial. However, should they dare to cherish wickedness and have rebellious hearts, they will run counter to heaven's constancy and violate human principle.

(Article 6)

For the first offence, merely hatching a rebellious plot was sufficient to establish guilt, but for the other two, the accused had to have committed a seditious or treasonable act. In all three cases, the punishment was decapitation, to be carried out immediately. The normal distinction between principals and accessories did not apply, and all suffered the same fate.

If either of the first two abominations had been committed, punishment didn't end with the execution of the defendant. Instead, punishment was also invoked on the criminal's entire extended family, as explained in Article 32:

Plotting rebellion and great sedition are criminal to the utmost degree of censure and extermination. They defile the whole family and property and the eradication of evil must reach to the roots.

In the case of plotting rebellion, 'collective prosecution' meant that the criminal's father and sons were strangled. Any sons under 15 were enslaved, as were the criminal's grandfather, great-grandfather and great-great-grandfather in the male line, grandsons, great-grandsons and great-great-grandsons in the male line, his brothers, his sons' concubines and any servants or slaves belonging to any of the above. All female relatives suffered enslavement or life exile instead. All their goods were confiscated by the state, and paternal uncles and nephews in the male line were exiled to a distance of 3000 li.

Collective prosecution also applied for other offences, including killing three members of a family, which was classed as depravity. The punishment was lighter than for plotting rebellion; principals and accessories were executed and their wives and sons were exiled to a distance of 2000 li.

According to the laws of the abominations, any offences against family or bureaucratic superiors were considered to be against the natural order and were therefore severely punished. Plotting to kill one's parent or paternal grandparent was punishable by death. The penalty for hitting a parent was death, while hitting a child was no crime at all.

Another provision, which had been enforced since the Han dynasty (206 BCE–220 CE), stated that a son who accused a parent of wrongdoing should be condemned to death if the accusation proved false. If it was true, however, the son didn't escape punishment; he was sentenced to three years of penal servitude and 100 blows with the heavy stick instead.

Plotting to kill a government superior would be penalized by a life in exile, whereas plotting against a person of equal rank was punishable merely by penal servitude. Within the government bureaucracy, if an official of the fifth rank hit an official of the third (and higher) rank, he would receive 60 blows with the heavy stick, instead of the usual 40 blows with the light stick for assaulting someone of equal rank. If the offender was a lowly official of the ninth rank, the punishment would be one year of penal servitude, and if he was a mere clerk with no rank, two years of penal servitude.

A HUSBAND WHO HIT HIS WIFE COMMITTED NO CRIME, BUT A WIFE WHO HIT HER HUSBAND FACED A YEAR IN PRISON.

Punishment according to status

The practice of punishment according to status extended throughout the Tang Code. High-ranking offenders received lighter punishments or escaped punishment altogether. Certain groups were granted special treatment; an offender from this category would have their punishment automatically reduced by one degree. For capital offences, application was made to the emperor to assign a lighter punishment at his discretion. Members of these privileged groups could not be tortured to extract a confession, and could not be convicted without the testimony of three witnesses.

Punishment for many crimes could be avoided by payment of a fine or by loss of rank, also employed as a punishment in itself. For lesser crimes, an offender was stripped of his position for one year, after which he could resume his office at a lower rank. For more serious crimes loss of rank was permanent. Although the Code recommended particularly harsh penalties for official corruption, in practice officials were exempt from the punishments stipulated in the Code for virtually all offences except the Ten Abominations.

The rank of the victim was also taken into account when sentencing an offender. Crimes against servants and bondsmen were generally punished one degree less severely, and crimes committed against slaves earned a penalty lessened by two degrees. Conversely, servants and bondsmen found guilty of a crime received punishment one degree more severe, for slaves penalties were two degrees more severe. A slave who assaulted a commoner so as to break a limb or put out an eye was executed, while a master who killed a slave without cause received no more than a year of penal servitude.

Other factors also came into play when a sentence was being decided. Before judgement could be pronounced, the offender had to confess to the crime. Trials were therefore geared towards extracting a confession from the accused, to the extent that torture was permitted and routinely employed. If an offender confessed his crime before a prosecution had been brought, he could often escape punishment, or if the crime was a capital one, he could escape the death sentence. However, this provision did not apply to crimes against the person, which had to be prosecuted, or to any of the Ten Abominations.

The generally heavy punishments set out in the Code were also mitigated for women, the very young and very old, and the mentally or physically disabled of all social classes. Those aged under seven, or 90 years or older, would usually escape the death penalty. Those aged 15 or younger, or 70 or above, could redeem themselves of all crimes except the most severe by payment of a fine, and were also exempt from torture, as were the mentally and physically disabled. Under another provision, an offender who was the sole supporter of aged or infirm parents would often have his death or prison sentence commuted.

JUDGE DEE

Di Renjie (630–700), better known to the world as Judge Dee, was a famous magistrate of the Tang era. Little is known of Di's actual cases, but he has lived on as a fictionalized character in the Chinese popular imagination for centuries, attaining much the same mythical status as Sherlock Holmes in the UK.

The fictional exploits of Di were first told in *Di Gong An*, a book written by an anonymous author in the 18th century. In it, Di solves three cases at once in a far-fetched plotline common to the majority of detective novels of the era, and was a wise and just magistrate.

In 1949, Sinophile Robert van Gulik translated *Di Gong An* as *The Celebrated Cases of Judge Dee*, and added to Dee's adventures by writing a successful series of Judge Dee novels. While Van Gulik updated Dee's sleuthing methods to fit in with the conventions of modern detective fiction, Di himself would have had less reputable methods at his disposal – spies, intimidation and torture were all legitimate ways of meeting out justice during the Tang period.

LEFT: A 19th-century Chinese criminal kneels prior to being decapitated by a sword. Attached to his hair is a sign showing his name and his offence. In the background a second criminal is carried away to meet a similar fate.

Doing what ought not to be done

Just in case any offences were not covered in the exhaustive and extremely specific Code, Article 450, entitled 'Doing what ought not to be done' served as a catch-all provision. Since all judgements had to be supported by the appropriate article of the Code, this gave magistrates some leeway to punish offenders on their own initiative.

However, the government did not want magistrates to interpret the law of their own accord: it wanted them merely to act as the automatic instruments of the law as explicitly set out in the Tang Code. Magistrates' rights were therefore severely restricted under Article 450. Punishments were limited to either 40 blows with the light stick or 80 blows with the heavy stick. All punishments greater than a beating had to be approved by higher authorities, and in the case of the death penalty, by the emperor himself.

CHAPTER FIVE

CORPORAL PUNISHMENT

Corporal punishment is punishment of the body, the most common methods being flogging, mutilation and amputation. Historically, it has been a punishment usually reserved for the low-born and often carried out in public.

Public humiliation is an important component that adds to the pain; the offender is exposed to the potential abuse or violence of a hostile crowd. In some cases shaming is also used as a punishment in itself.

FLOGGING

The ancient Romans were especially fond of flogging their slaves. Roman poet Horace (65 BCE–8 CE) wrote that when whipping a slave it was not uncommon for the executioner to collapse from exhaustion before the job was finished. Minor offences were punished with a flat leather strop called a *ferula*; more severe was the *scutica*, which was made of strips of stiff parchment. There was also an ox-hide cart-whip and, most feared of all, the *flagellum*, which was also used as a weapon in the gladiatorial arena. This consisted of long ox-hide thongs, which were either knotted or weighted with slivers of bone, metal balls or hooks. This weapon was the precursor to the famous 'cat o'nine tails' later favoured by the British navy.

The Romans also started the tradition of public flogging, when those convicted of capital crimes were whipped on the way to their place of execution, as Jesus was on the way to his crucifixion. This was perhaps the origin of the English practice of 'whipping at the cart's tail', where an offender was tied to the back of a cart and whipped as he was led through the town. The practice was long established before Henry VIII introduced the Act Against Vagrants (known as the 'Whipping Act') in 1530. This Act stated that vagrants were to be 'carried to some market town nearby … and there tied to the end

LEFT: A French magazine illustration from 1907 depicts hard labour on the treadmill and flogging with the cat o' nine tails in a British penal institution.

ABOVE: A grim example or public entertainment? Onlookers watch a public whipping in London's Sessions House Yard, 1745, an engraving from the *Newgate Calendar*.

of a cart naked and beaten with whips [throughout the town] … till the body shall be bloody by reason of such whipping'.

There was usually no specified number of strokes; the offender received as many as could be given while going through the town. In 1736, the gravedigger of St. Dunstan's in Stepney, east London, was sentenced to a whipping through the town for stealing bodies and selling them to a private surgeon. The crowd was so outraged at this offence that they paid the executioner, John Hooper, to lead the horses slowly so that the gravedigger received hundreds of lashes.

When the Inquisition descended on a town looking for heretics, they generally imposed a 30-day 'grace period' in which heretics could come forward and confess. For this they would receive the punishment of penance, rather than face the gruesome prospect of torture and burning at the stake. Although it was the lightest punishment imposed by the Inquisition, this penalty was no easy option. The penitent was obliged to strip and appear in church on Sunday carrying a rod. At a given point in the Mass, the priest would break off from the service to whip the penitent in front of the assembled congregation.

The punishment did not end there. On the first Sunday of every month, the penitent was also obliged to visit every house where he had met with other heretics and be whipped at each one. Finally, on feast days the penitent accompanied the solemn processions and was whipped through the town. The whippings continued regularly until the Inquisitor who had imposed the sentence released the heretic. In practice, Inquisitors tended to descend on a town for a few months and then move on, returning years later, if at all. Forgotten penitents could easily find themselves condemned to a lifetime of whipping.

Flogging was meted out for a range of offences. In 18th-century England, theft of goods worth more than 12 pence was punished by flogging; in 1772 a thief was whipped around Covent Garden for stealing a bunch of radishes. Women as well as men were whipped, usually for adultery or prostitution. In Aberdeen in 1640 Margaret Warrack was flogged for 'fornication', and in 1653 two Quaker preachers, Mary Fisher and Elizabeth Williams, were found guilty of being 'whores' and were whipped at the market cross in Cambridge.

By the end of the 18th century, public flogging had declined in England due to the increasing use of transportation as a penalty and the gradual emergence of more enlightened notions of punishment. Jeremy Bentham wrote in the 1770s that 'mutilations may now be considered as banished from the penal code of Great Britain.' But Europeans had no such scruples when it came to their colonies. Flogging, along with mutilation, branding and torture all survived in the New World, African and Asian colonies for at least another 100 years.

THE WHIPPING OF THE QUAKER WOMEN

Preaching the Quaker doctrine could be heavily punished. In 1662, three New Hampshire Quakers, Ann Coleman, Mary Tompkins and Alice Ambrose, were sentenced to be whipped at the cart's tail through 11 towns, receiving 10 strokes apiece in each town. This was a journey of some 80 miles through snowbound winter roads that would take several days to complete.

On a particularly cold day the women were stripped to the waist and whipped through Dover, then taken by cart to Hampton, which they reached at nightfall. The next morning they were whipped and conveyed to Salisbury where they received their third flogging. At this point, a Dr Walter Barefoot of Salisbury came to the women's assistance. He had himself sworn in as deputy, took possession of the warrant and ended the punishment.

The event was immortalized in a rather tedious poem by John Greenleaf Whittier:

'How They Drove the Quaker Women from Dover'

The tossing spray of Cochecho's falls
Hardened to ice on its icy walls,
As through Dover town, in the chill gray dawn,
Three women passed, at the cart tail drawn,
Bared to the waist, for the north wind's grip
And keener sting of the constables whip
The blood that followed each hissing blow
Froze as it sprinkled the winter snow.
Priest and ruler, boy and maiden
Followed the dismal cavalcade;
And from door and window, open thrown,
Looked and wondered, gaffer and crone.

Slaves in the American south had no legal protection at all. In South Carolina, the law stated that slaves were not 'within the peace of the state and therefore the peace of the state is not broken by an assault and battery on him'. Samuel Gridley Howe observed a slave woman being flogged in a New Orleans jail he visited in 1846. Naked below the waist, she was tied face down to a board:

By her side stood a huge Negro with a long whip, which he applied with dreadful power and wonderful precision. Every stroke brought away a strip of skin, which clung to the lash or fell quivering on the pavement, while the blood followed after it.

BELOW: An illustration entitled "The Mode of Flogging Slaves" from the 1825 book *West Indies As They Are*, showing slaves restraining and beating another slave as their master looks on.

Her flesh became a livid and bloody mass of raw and quivering muscle. … It was with the greatest difficulty I refrained from springing upon the torturer and arresting his lash; but alas! What could I do but turn aside to hide my tears for the sufferer and my blushes for humanity?

Such punishments were not unusual, as Howe observed: 'This was a public and regularly organized prison; the punishment was one recognized and authorized by the law.' Slave owners who killed their slaves during hard physical punishment faced no penalty. Prosecutions against slave owners were rare, and even if successful the worst that could befall the owners was to be forced to free their slaves.

A British House of Commons committee was told in 1814 of the case of a Mr Huggins who subjected '21 of his slaves, men, and women, to upwards of 3000 lashes of the cartwhip' in the marketplace of Nevis, Jamaica. One of the women suffered 291 lashes and one of the men no less than 365.

In another case, in 1829 the Reverend G.W. Bridges personally flogged his Jamaican cook until she was a 'mass of lacerated flesh and gore' for the offence of killing a turkey for a dinner guest who failed to show up. Bridges was summoned to court, but despite witnesses and the evidence of the woman's injuries, he was acquitted.

The flogging of slaves was routine, not merely to punish offences but to demonstrate the owner's authority and to curb insubordination. In Jamaica, as in other colonies, slaves were 'bowsed out' (as the practice was referred to in seafaring slang) – the victim was strung up by the wrists and ankles and stretched by a rope and pulley. The slaves were then whipped to 'beat out the bad blood', or in other words, beaten into submission.

BENTHAM'S FLOGGING MACHINE

Although a prominent Enlightenment thinker, philosopher and legal reformer Jeremy Bentham was not against flogging per se; he was more concerned by the lack of consistency of the punishment. The severity of a criminal's admonishment was entirely dependent on the strength, build and nature of the executioner; 20 lashes at the hands of a small, drunken executioner were nothing compared to 20 strokes dished out by a strong and mean one. For this reason, in his book *The Rationale of Punishment*, which was written in 1770s and was published in 1830, Bentham proposed the use of a rotary flogging machine that would lash every offender with exactly the same degree of force:

Of all these different modes of punishment, whipping is the most frequently in use; but in whipping not even the qualities of the instrument are ascertained by written law: while the quantity of force to be employed in its application is altogether entrusted to the caprice of the executioner. He may make the punishment as trifling or as severe as he pleases. …

The following contrivance would, in a measure, obviate this inconvenience. A machine might be made, which should put in motion certain elastic rods of cane or whalebone, the number and size of which might be determined by the law: the body of the delinquent might be subjected to the strokes of these rods, and the force and rapidity with which they should be applied, might be prescribed by the Judge: thus everything which is arbitrary might be removed.

A public officer, of more responsible character than the common executioner, might preside over the infliction of the punishment; and when there were many delinquents to be punished, his time might be saved, and the terror of the scene heightened, without increasing the actual suffering, by increasing the number of the machines, and subjecting all the offenders to punishment at the same time.

RIGHT: Spain, 1937 –
a Republican soldier
suspected of treachery is
flogged before later being
shot under harsh
military law.

Even after the ending of slavery, black Americans were not free from the threat of flogging. As late as 1851 a provision in Yankee Boston stated that blacks found on the streets at night were liable to be arrested and given 39 lashes, a punishment presumably derived from the Biblical injunction against giving more than 40 strokes.

Flogging today

The practice of flogging also outlasted imperialism in other colonies. When Singapore became a British colony in 1834, English criminal law was applied, which included provisions for judicial flogging. Flogging was imposed for such crimes as begging, distributing pornography, treason and robbery with violence. On attaining independence in 1948, Singapore retained corporal punishment in its own legal code and in 1965 the number of offences liable to flogging was increased. There are currently 30 mandatory flogging offences, including attempted murder, rape, armed robbery, drug trafficking, immigration offences and vandalism.

The case of 18-year-old American Michael Fay, a Singapore resident who was sentenced in 1994 to four months in jail, a $2,230 fine and six lashes for allegedly spray-painting two cars attracted the attention of the world's media. Fay later maintained that he was innocent and that the confession he signed two days after his arrest was made under duress. No spray-cans or other evidence were found in Fay's possession, and he was sentenced on the strength of a dubious statement made by another young man also accused of vandalism, who had named Fay as the real culprit. A storm of international protest, including an appeal from President Clinton, succeeded in reducing the sentence from six lashes to four, but not in commuting the sentence. On the morning of 5 May 1994, Fay's mother and lawyer visited him at Queenstown Remand Centre and told him that his sentence had been reduced but that it would still go ahead, although they had not been told when. After the visit, Fay was escorted back to his cell and a few minutes later the prison guards rounded up the 10 prisoners, including Fay, who were to be caned.

ABOVE: Singapore, March 1994: Michael Fay (right) arrives at court to face trial for vandalism. Fay was found guilty and sentenced to prison, a fine and six lashes for the crime of spray-painting a car.

According to the legal provisions, a doctor and three prison officers were waiting when Fay's turn in the caning room came. The doctor took Fay's pulse and ensured that he was fit to receive his punishment. Fay was then led to an A-shaped wooden frame and asked to remove his shorts and bend over the frame. An officer shackled his ankles and wrists to it and a pillow was placed above his buttocks to protect his spine and kidneys should a stroke go astray. A prison officer, who, it later emerged, was also a martial arts expert, administered the four lashes to Fay's bare buttocks with a 1.2 m (47 in) long, 13 mm (½ in) thick rattan cane that had been soaked in brine. The officer raised the cane above his head and brought it down with full force four times, pausing between each stroke for a signal from the doctor to continue. The punishment took less than a minute.

Fay's sentence of six lashes was lenient by Singapore standards; a boy found guilty of vandalism the week before Fay was sentenced to 12 lashes by the same judge. Francis Seow, former Singapore Solicitor General, expressed the view of most Singaporeans when he said in a radio interview about the Fay case: 'Well, you see, the proof of the pudding lies in the eating. ... I mean, you look at Singapore today. You can walk the streets quite happily without fear of being mugged, assaulted, raped, or robbed, and look what's going on in America.'

Both Iran and Saudi Arabia also rely heavily on flogging to discipline their errant citizens. A BBC news report in December 2002 revealed that, contrary to the government's claims of a more liberal interpretation of the laws, the strictest possible interpretation of Sharia was being implemented in Iran and few social restrictions – if any at all – had been lifted. An undercover reporter discovered that juveniles were also receiving sentences of flogging. A group of teenage boys and girls had recently been given 80 lashes each simply for being in the same house together, in contravention of Iran's strict sexual segregation laws.

RIGHT: A Singapore executioner demonstrates the correct flogging technique on a dummy. Regulations state that blows are struck with a 1.2m-long rattan cane raised above the head and brought down full force on the prisoner's bare buttocks.

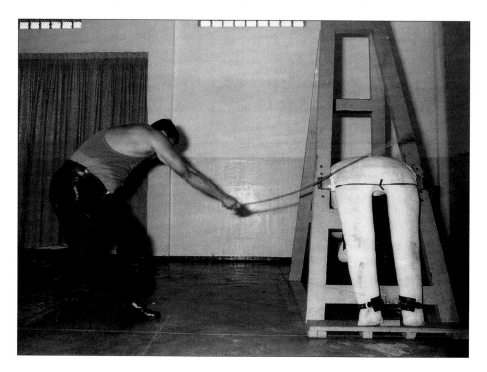

Iranian sentences are nothing compared to those in Saudi Arabia. In August 2002, a Jeddah court handed down a sentence of seven years' imprisonment and 1680 lashes to a habitual car thief. The 1680 lashes were to be administered in 42 instalments, with an interval of seven days between sessions. In the same month, a woman was sentenced to 15 years in jail and an incredible 5000 lashes to be administered over several years for running a prostitution ring in Medina.

BRANDING AND MUTILATION

The scars from a whipping might last a lifetime, but at least the criminal had a chance of hiding the evidence of past misdemeanours. Like branding, mutilation is a permanent punishment for the offender. It marked a criminal out for life, leaving him subject to constant discrimination and violence.

Branding

The first recorded use of branding was by the Babylonians, where it was used to punish those who slandered married women or priestesses. The Romans branded runaway slaves on the forehead with 'F' for *fugitivus*. Thieves, too, were often branded. Brands were usually applied to the forehead.

In medieval England, criminals had letters representing the crimes they committed branded on the face or body. 'T' denoted a thief, 'B' meant a blasphemer, 'SL' stood for seditious libeller, 'P' for perjurer and 'F' for fraymaker (someone who caused a disturbance in church). In Scotland, the usual practice was branding the offender's cheek with a red-hot key.

Branding was intended to forewarn neighbours of a criminal threat as branded criminals could be easily identified – an important factor in an age when it was difficult to verify identity. For the criminal, branding was a lifelong punishment, subjecting him to harassment and violence, and rendering him unemployable, thus forcing him once more into a life of crime. By the 14th century, branding was on the wane, and was replaced by hanging for major offences and the pillory or flogging for minor ones.

In the 17th century, branding was rare but was still used for seditious libel and blasphemy. Laws passed against Quakers in England and the American colonies ordered them to be branded and to be mutilated on the tongue – the organ they had used to spread their blasphemous notions. In 1656 in Bristol Quaker preacher James Naylor was convicted of making himself an object of worship among the people. He was ordered to be pilloried, whipped and to have his tongue pierced by a hot iron, thereby rendering him speechless. He then had 'B' for blasphemer branded on his forehead and was sentenced to imprisonment with hard labour. Branding was outlawed in England in 1829.

TATTOOING APPEARED AS VERY MUCH AN UNOFFICIAL PUNISHMENT IN A CASE FROM INDIA IN THE 1990s. COMPENSATION WAS PAID BY THE COURTS TO FOUR PUNJABI WOMEN WHO WERE CONVICTED OF PICKPOCKETING AND WHO HAD HAD THE WORD 'THIEF' TATTOOED ON THEIR FACES BY MEMBERS OF THE STATE POLICE.

RIGHT: In late 18th century London, a convicted criminal is branded on the hand at the New Sessions House. Branding was not abolished in England until 1829.

RIGHT: In late 18th century London, a convicted criminal is branded on the hand at the New Sessions House. Branding was not abolished in England until 1829.

Mutilation

In some cases mutilation took things one step further from branding by disabling an offender as well as inflicting a permanent and visible reminder of his crime upon him and those around him. Mutilation has been used as a punishment since at least the first century, when it was set down in the Indian Laws of Manu for crimes committed by lower castes against their superiors or the community at large. The Babylonian Code of Hammurabi famously decrees sympathetic amputation, 'an eye for an eye' and this provision was retained in the Hebrew and Roman legal codes. Sharia calls for theft to be punished by amputation of the hand, a punishment that is still carried out today in Islamic countries.

Mutilation was already established in continental Europe when William the Conqueror introduced it to England after 1066, declaring it a more

LAWS AGAINST QUAKERS

A General Court Held at Boston, the Fourteenth of October, 1657, stated:

And it is further ordered, that if any Quaker or Quakers shall presume, after they have once suffered what the law requires, to come into this jurisdiction, every such male Quaker shall, for the first offence, have one of his ears cut off, and be kept at work in the House of Correction, until he can be sent away at his own charge; and for the second offence, shall have his other ear cut off; and every woman Quaker, that has suffered the law here, that shall presume to come into this jurisdiction, shall be severely whipped, and kept at the House of Correction at work, until she be sent away at her own charge, and so also for her coming again, she shall be alike used as aforesaid.

And for every Quaker, he or she, that shall a third time herein again offend, they shall have their tongues bored through with a hot iron, and be kept at the House of Correction close to work, until they be sent away at their own charge.

BELOW: London, 17 December 1656: after two hours in the pillory, Quaker preacher James Naylor is whipped through the town (left) before he is branded and his tongue bored through with a red-hot poker.

effective deterrent than hanging. Robbery and arson were punished by amputation of the right foot and having the eyes gouged. Both splitting of noses and severing of ears were ordered fairly indiscriminately for quite a variety of crimes.

Throughout history, mutilation has usually been carried out in public, providing both a deterrent and a somewhat bloodthirsty day out for the watching crowd. In England, judicial mutilations were often performed while the offender was in the pillory or stocks. The common punishment of splitting or cutting off the ear was frequently carried out by nailing the offender's ear to the pillory. When the offender was later released the ear would be ripped off. In the 13th century, petty thieves were punished by thumb amputation, and mutilation was still in use in Henry VIII's reign, when non-attendance at church earned the absentee a severed ear. Mutilation had largely died out by the time that Elizabeth I reintroduced it for the crime of seditious libel. The new law caused something of a sensation and was clearly intended as a 'get tough' policy aimed at her political opponents.

RIGHT: An illustration from Foxe's *Book of Martyrs* depicts prisoner Daniel Rambant chained up in his cell as his fingers and toes are cut off.

The same kind of political motives that drove Elizabeth I can be seen in the modern application of mutilation in countries and regions newly subject to Sharia law. Between 1999 and 2002, 12 states in northern Nigeria adopted Sharia and began to impose sentences of amputation. The BBC reported that in 2001 in the state of Soloko a man had his right hand amputated for stealing a goat worth about $40 and another man suffered the same fate for stealing a bicycle. Amputation is most routinely carried out in Saudi Arabia; Amnesty International estimates that 90 judicial amputations were carried out there between 1981 and 1999.

SHAMING: THE PILLORY AND THE STOCKS

The pillory and the stocks represented a diverse method of discipline by ensuring that the shame and discrimination suffered by a criminal became his direct punishment. The pillory and stocks are wooden structures to which an offender is attached for public shaming. In the stocks, the offender sits on the ground with his legs in front of him and his ankles secured. In the pillory, the offender stands, with his neck and wrists secured. Thought to have originated in England in the 13th century, these devices were later exported to other European countries and were taken by the Pilgrim Fathers to the new settlements in America. Stocks were a staple of virtually every village green in England, while the pillory was more of an urban punishment and were usually placed at busy crossroads for maximum visibility.

Although the confinement was no doubt uncomfortable and the public display humiliating, the precise punishment the offender received depended entirely on the crowd. Offenders were insulted, abused and deluged with missiles, which could include rotten fruits and vegetables, eggs, dead rats, stones or animal or human excrement, depending on the mood of the crowd and the popularity of the offender. This meant that in some cases, a sentence to the stocks or pillory amounted to the death penalty. In 1756 Stephen MacDaniel, James Salmon, John Berry and James Egan were found guilty of giving false evidence that had sent two men to the gallows. They were each sentenced to spend an hour in the pillory at Smithfield in London. An hour was punishment enough as the enraged crowd threw missiles including sticks, stones and oyster shells. Egan was dead by the time his hour was up, his skull cracked by a stone. The other three died of their injuries a few days later at Newgate prison.

By the same token, if the public felt the offence was trivial the offender could escape injury. A man pilloried at Cheapside in 1738 for refusing to pay the government duty on soap was cheered throughout his stint. In 1704, author Daniel Defoe was pilloried for satirizing the government. He spent a pleasant hour at Charing Cross surrounded by supporters who plied him with food and drink and showered him with flowers.

The Chinese used a version of the pillory called the *cangue,* a wide, hinged wooden board with a hole for the offender's neck, and sometimes hands too. Although they were not attached to a fixed structure, offenders were still unable to defend themselves against attack. A scroll proclaiming the offence the person had committed was pinned to the cangue and victims were paraded through the street for public scorn and ridicule.

EVEN WHEN EMPTY, THE PROMINENTLY DISPLAYED STOCKS AND PILLORY WERE A POWERFUL VISUAL SYMBOL OF AUTHORITY.

The return of shaming

Although not a punishment inflicted directly on the body, shaming could inflict a double blow on the criminal by leaving them vulnerable to assault from those around them, and inflicting a form of mental suffering also. The classic model of shaming is Nathaniel Hawthorne's novel *The Scarlet Letter*, in which the adulteress Hester Prynne is made to wear a scarlet letter 'A' around her neck. Judges in 21st-century Texas have tried to recreate the Puritan New England of Hawthorne's novel by reintroducing public shaming.

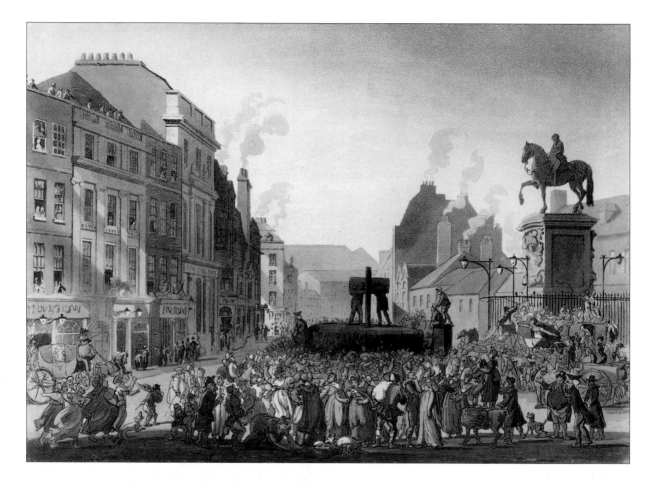

ABOVE: A crowd around the pillory at London's Charing Cross, as recorded by the 18th-century cartoonist Thomas Rowlandson. Public punishments and executions were a good 'day out', with stalls and entertainers adding to the carnival atmosphere.

The shaming punishments came about after a 1999 provision in Texas law ordered probationers to give notice of their offence 'in any manner required by the judge'. One of the framers of that legislation, Judge Ted Poe of Harris County District Court in Houston, has since handed down more than 300 'public notice' sentences.

These have included making a man who beat his wife apologize on the steps of City Hall and ordering a drunk driver to stand in front of a bar with the sign: 'I killed two people while driving drunk.' In 2001, district judge J. Manuel Bañales of Corpus Christi in southern Texas ordered 15 sex offenders on probation to place warning signs in their front yards reading: 'Danger, Registered Sex Offender Lives Here.' The offenders were also required to display a matching bumper sticker on their cars and to display a sign even when riding in a friend's car.

There is considerable opposition to these shaming sentences on the grounds that it contravenes the Eighth Amendment prohibition of 'cruel and unusual punishment'. For all the lofty sentiments about protecting the community, judges who impose shaming sentences know that for the offender the real punishment is harassment and violence from their neighbours. Many of the offenders 'named and shamed' by Bañales have been insulted, attacked and had their property destroyed. It was reported that the very first offender Bañales sentenced in his first batch of 15 sex offenders had only six weeks to go before the end of his parole and had, in the view of his psychologist, been completely rehabilitated.

Another of the 15 had been harassed and thrown out of his apartment, and was lying in a flophouse and described as suicidal. *Texas Monthly* revealed that offenders' neighbours were prompted by fear and moral panic to try to drive them out and property prices collapsed anywhere near a publicly proclaimed sex offender.

The pillory and stocks were popular punishments with the authorities because they were cheap to administer; the public was only to happy to carry out the punishment, thus saving the authorities much of the expense. The same applies to modern shaming sentences, which amount to a licence for vigilantism.

Corporal punishment today

At the beginning of the 21st century, corporal punishment is no longer a legal sanction in most countries around the world. Many countries have also added laws banning corporal punishment in schools or even parents smacking their own children. At the same time, in some countries corporal punishment has been retained and even extended.

In some countries, flogging is a hangover from a colonial past, retained long after the colonizers had abolished it as a legal penalty. Amputation has also been on the increase in the past ten or twenty years as more states and nations have adopted a strict and literal reading of Sharia law.

BELOW: Coshocton, Ohio, United States, 2001 – Jason Householder (left) and John Stockum were given the choice of 60 days in jail or an hour walking down Main Street in women's clothing as their sentence for throwing beer bottles at a woman in a car.

CHAPTER SIX

THROWING AWAY THE KEY: IMPRISONMENT

A lthough imprisonment has been used as a punishment since ancient times, the most common means of dealing with offenders were execution and corporal punishment. The 18th century heralded the gradual reversal of this trend and the beginnings of the modern European penal system. French philosopher Michel Foucault (1926–84), illustrated the momentous nature of this change in the introduction to his classic study of prisons *Discipline and Punish*. He begins with a detailed description of the public execution of Robert-François Damiens in Paris in 1757. Damiens was sentenced to be publicly quartered for the attempted assassination of King Louis XV. The judgement stated that he was to be:

> ... taken ... to the Place de Grève, where, on a scaffold that will be erected there, the flesh will be torn from his breasts, arms, thighs and calves with red-hot pincers, his right hand, holding the knife with which he committed the said parricide [killing of a parent or other close relative], burnt with sulphur, and, on those places where the flesh will be torn away, poured molten lead, boiling oil, burning resin, wax and sulphur melted together and then his body drawn and quartered by four horses and his limbs and his body consumed by fire, reduced to ashes and his ashes thrown to the winds.

The sentence proved particularly difficult to carry out, as described in an account written by Bouton, an officer of the watch. First of all, the sulphur would not light and gave off little heat. Then the red-hot pincers could not pull off Damiens' flesh and merely left burn marks 'about the size of a six-

LEFT: Inmates line up at a military-style 'boot camp' in Georgia. Boot camps are an alternative to prison sentences, designed to scare young people away from reoffending. Though boot camps are popular with voters looking for action on crime, they do little to rehabilitate offenders unless supplemented by support, education and training.

pound crown piece'. The quartering was bungled too. A horse was attached to each limb and was driven forward by an executioner, but to no avail: Damiens remained firmly in one piece. Eventually, the executioners were ordered to cut off his limbs.

Foucault contrasts this gruesome public spectacle with a punishment from just 80 years later – extracts from a prison timetable issued in Paris that prescribed every minute of the prisoners' day:

Article 18. Rising. At the first drum-roll, the prisoners must rise and dress in silence, as the supervisor opens the cell doors. At the second drum-roll, they must be dressed and make their beds. At the third, they must line up and proceed to the chapel for morning prayer. …

Article 20. Work. At a quarter to six in the summer, a quarter to seven in winter, the prisoners go down into the courtyard where they must wash their hands and faces, and receive their first ration of bread. Immediately afterwards, they form into work teams and go off to work, which must begin at six in summer and seven in winter. …

Article 27. At seven o'clock in the summer, at eight in winter, work stops; bread is distributed for the last time in the workshops. For a quarter of an hour one of the prisoners or supervisors reads a passage from some instructive or uplifting work. This is followed by evening prayer. …

The account of Damiens' execution strikes us as medieval, and the 1830s prison schedule as undoubtedly modern. Public torture has been replaced by imprisonment and the focus of punishment, despite a harsh prison regime, has shifted from the body to the mind.

Only 80 years separates the two passages quoted by Foucault, but the transition had in fact already begun by 1757. Such gruesome public displays had all but disappeared by then; the French authorities had chosen to punish Damiens by reviving the method of execution used for the previous attempted regicide, François Ravillac, in 1610. No such punishment had been tried for 150 years and it never would be again.

BELOW: French philosopher, historian and critic Michel Foucault. In his history of the European prison, *Discipline and Punish*, Foucault examined how the rise of prisons in the 18th century contributed to the formation of the modern world view.

ENLIGHTENED THINKING

By 1757, the new social ideas that would lead before the end of the century to revolutions in France and America had already begun to effect a permanent change in social attitudes. Enlightenment philosophers like Voltaire (1694–1778), Jean-Jacques Rousseau (1712–78) and John Locke (1632–1704) fuelled social change with their belief in human potential, free will and the innate goodness of man. Rousseau wrote of the 'social contract' that bound an individual and society together, and Locke wrote of government 'by consent of the governed'. This new school of philosophers spoke out against torture and capital punishment, which to them represented the barbarism of a bygone age that was contrary to all reason and humanity.

As these new ideas began to influence European societies, attitudes towards punishment changed. It was believed that punishment should be just enough to deter and should be predictable and proportional to the crime. Prison conformed perfectly to these rational Enlightenment ideas. The length of a

ABOVE: A 1611 engraving of the courtyard of Rasphuis prison in Amsterdam. One prisoner is being flogged while a guard supervises two other prisoners sawing wood.

ABOVE: Milanese aristocrat Cesare Beccaria published his treatise *On Crimes and Punishments* privately for a local intellectual society but his book changed the course of penal history. Painfully shy Beccaria shunned the fame his book brought him and chose to end his days in the relative obscurity of a local government post.

prison sentence would be preordained by laws to make sure that the accused did not fall victim to the whim of a capricious judge. During the 18th century, previously horrific prison conditions were improved to conform to the emerging notions of universal human rights. For the first time, prison regimes hinted at the possibility of reform and rehabilitation of offenders.

A short treatise written by Italian Cesare Beccaria (1738–1794), *On Crimes and Punishments* (1764), is perhaps the most influential reform tract ever published. Beccaria wrote the piece at the request of the brothers Pietro and Alessandro Verri who led the radical intellectual circle known as the Academy of Fists, of which Beccaria was a member. Beccaria had no direct knowledge of the law but the brothers were superbly placed to supply all the factual information that he lacked: Pietro was in the process of writing a history of torture and Alessandro was a prison official.

On Crimes and Punishments was an immediate success, running to several editions, and was soon translated into French and English. Beccaria's early admirers included Catherine the Great of Russia and Maria Theresa of Austria-Hungary and he was cited in the writings of Voltaire, Thomas Jefferson and John Adams.

The celebrated Beccaria was duly invited to Paris to meet the great thinkers of the day, an invitation that the painfully shy author reluctantly accepted. Beccaria made a poor impression, to say the least. As Henry Paolucci puts it in the introduction to his 1963 edition of *On Crimes and Punishments*, the French intellectuals thought Beccaria 'a childish imbecile without backbone and incapable of living away from his mother'.

Beccaria's brief tract applied Enlightenment theories to an analysis of the existing legal and penal institutions. He found a cruel and irrational system where the laws were unclear and the punishments arbitrary and excessive. Beccaria's persuasive and carefully reasoned argument called for radical reform: public trials, the ending of torture and capital punishment and the adoption of punishments that are swift and proportionate to the crime.

Beccaria believed that the individual should give up as few freedoms as possible; he should have to relinquish only those as are absolutely necessary for maintaining the social contract. Society, in turn, had the right to punish a citizen only to the degree necessary for the protection of public order:

> All that extends beyond this, is abuse, not justice. Observe that by justice I understand nothing more than that bond which is necessary to keep the interest of individuals united, without which men would return to their original state of barbarity. All punishments which exceed the necessity of preserving this bond are in their nature unjust.

Thus, from his utilitarian point of view, Beccaria claimed that torture and executions were not only barbarous but ineffective also:

> What are, in general, the proper punishments for crimes? Is the punishment of death really useful, or necessary for the safety or good order of society? Are tortures and torments consistent with justice, or do they answer the end proposed by the laws? Which is the best method of preventing crimes?…

> …The intent of punishments is not to torment a sensible being, nor to undo a crime already committed. The end of punishment, therefore, is no other than to prevent the criminal from doing further injury to society, and to prevent others from committing the like offence.

It was, Beccaria argued, the certainty not the severity of punishment that should act as a deterrent. It was probably the first time that any serious challenge had been made to the notion that punishment naturally leads to maximum deterrence.

'Enlightened self-interest'

The son of a prominent London lawyer, Jeremy Bentham (1748–1832) seemed destined for a brilliant legal career when he was called to the bar in 1772. But his personal experiences convinced Bentham to take a different path instead. Having brought a court action and discovered that, 'it

BELOW: Jeremy Bentham, English philosopher and social reformer. In his long life, Bentham published over 80 books, championing, among other things, prison reform, universal male and female suffrage, free education and the legalization of homosexuality.

took three times as long, and was three times more expensive, than it should,' he decided to devote his life to analysing and reforming the English legal system. Bentham's disillusionment was fed by the writings of legal theorists such as Hume, Helvetius and Beccaria and the political pamphleteer Joseph Priestley, in whose pages Bentham first encountered the phrase 'the greatest happiness of the greatest number', which was to become the central tenet of his theory of utilitarianism.

Like Beccaria, Bentham believed that a crime could be prevented by ensuring that the strength of the penalty outweighed the pleasure gained by committing the crime. Beccaria wondered if such a strict mathematical formula could usefully be applied to the complexities of human criminal behaviour; Bentham attempted to do just that. In his *Introduction to the Principles of Morals and Legislation*, (1789), Bentham proposed a 'hedonic calculus', a method of measuring the total pain and pleasure produced by an act, which could then be used to determine the minimum deterrent needed to prevent that crime.

According to Bentham, human beings act according to 'enlightened self-interest'; they attempt to maximize their pleasure and minimize their pain. Thus, argued Bentham, enlightened self-interest was the only true basis for morality, not an external moral or religious code, nor a set of ancient laws: 'The greatest happiness of the greatest number is the foundation of morals and legislation.'

According to Bentham's theory, troublesome considerations such as sympathy or intent were irrelevant, as were any vague notions about natural rights or the social contract.

Bentham's 'mathematical' view of society is an uncompromising one and his analysis of human motives was regarded as too simplistic even when judged according to the crude standards of 18th century psychology. As Bentham's contemporary and social critic William Hazlitt put it: 'Bentham has lived for the past 40 years in a house in Westminster … reducing law to a system and the mind of man to a machine.'

Critics also seized upon Bentham's dense writing style, which being highly technical and peppered with peculiar Latinate coinages such as 'ipsedixitism', made few concessions to readability. 'He writes a language of his own that darkens knowledge,' said Hazlitt. 'His works have been translated into French – they ought to be translated into English,' quipped Hazlitt, continuing: 'It is not mere verbiage, but has a great deal of acuteness and meaning in it, which you would be glad to pick out if you could.' Marx was even less charitable, deeming Bentham 'a genius by way of bourgeois stupidity'. Despite this treatment by his critics, Bentham was to make a lasting

> 'THE GREATEST HAPPINESS OF THE GREATEST NUMBER IS THE FOUNDATION OF MORALS AND LEGISLATION.'
> —JEREMY BENTHAM

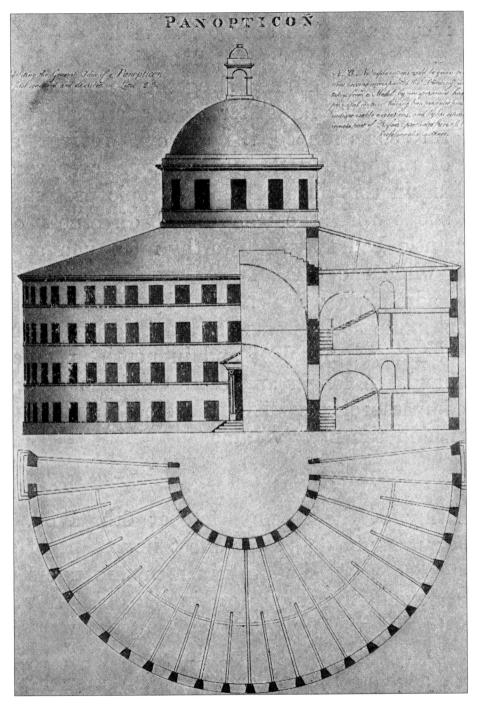

PANOPTICON.

LEFT: Bentham's plan for the Panopticon, a circular cell block built around a central observation tower. Though no Panopticon was ever built in Bentham's lifetime, the design was incorporated into many 19th- and 20th-century American penitentiaries.

contribution to the modern penal system with his plans for the 'Panopticon'. This was his name for a prison built with cells arranged in a circle around a central watchtower so that they could be observed at all times. This would have the effect of making prisoners feel like they are permanently under observation, even if not every individual cell is being watched at all times. As Foucault put it:

> The major effect of the Panopticon was to induce in the inmate a state of conscious and permanent visibility that assures the automatic functioning of power. So to arrange things that the surveillance is permanent in its effects even if it is discontinuous in its action; … that this architectural apparatus should be a machine for creating and sustaining a power relation independent of the person who exercises it.
>
> (Foucault, *Discipline and Punish*)

RIGHT: The last circular cell block in use in the United States, F House at Stateville Correctional Center near Joliet, Illinois, which was built in 1919. Guards in the central tower have an unrestricted view into each of the cells.

Bentham convinced the British government to let him build and run such an institution, but the project failed to get off the ground and was abandoned. Finally, in 1842, 10 years after Bentham's death, a modified version of the Panopticon was built at Pentonville prison in London. It held 520 prisoners in identical cells, in four wings radiating out from a central point. Strict separation was maintained at all times: prisoners were hooded when outside their cells and even the chapel was fitted with individual pens to prevent any contact.

The idea of the Panopticon was enthusiastically taken up in the state penitentiaries of the United States, which used the design well into the 20th century. The last remaining circular cell block in use in the United States today is F House at Stateville Correctional Center near Joliet, Illinois.

The rigours of prison life

Although many writers wrote about prison reform, few actually investigated the realities of prison life by visiting them. In Europe prisons were privately run and the owners' primary motivation was profit. This led to many cost-cutting measures that reduced the owners' overheads while increasing the inmates' discomfort. For instance, some prisoners were manacled in irons weighing as much as 18kg (40lb) and many were chained together so as to reduce the need for wardens and thereby save money. Little distinction was made between convicted criminals, debtors and those awaiting trial; they all suffered the same appalling living conditions. Prisoners were herded together in large cells without heating, bedding or sanitation. Cells were often underground, so depriving the inmate of light or fresh air. In such conditions vermin and disease were rife. In 1759 it was estimated that one in four prisoners died in jail each year, amounting to 5000 deaths.

Prisoners were also subject to more direct forms of punishment than their inhospitable environment. In some prisons, incarceration equated torture. In the Tower of London, the cell known as 'Little Ease' measured just 1.2 m^2

THE AUTO-ICON

In the main building of University College, London stands the 'Auto-Icon', a wooden cabinet containing Jeremy Bentham's preserved (and clothed) skeleton surmounted by a wax head. Eccentric in death as in life, Bentham requested that his skeleton be preserved in his will. He had originally intended for his head to be displayed too, but unfortunately the preservation of the head went wrong, leaving him with an unattractive expression, so a wax substitute was made.

Legends about the Auto-Icon abound; one story says that for the last 10 years of his life Bentham carried the glass eyes that were intended to adorn his skull around in his pocket. These glass eyes, along with his skull, were originally displayed at his feet in the cabinet, but this proved too great a temptation for the students of rival university, King's College, London. The skull was frequently stolen, one time ending up (so another story goes), in a left-luggage locker at Aberdeen station. The skull was subsequently removed to the UCL vaults. But perhaps the most intriguing legend states that the Auto-Icon is wheeled in to attend meetings of the College Council, where its attendance is noted in the minutes with the words 'Jeremy Bentham – present but not voting'.

(4 sq ft), making it impossible for the prisoner to sit or lie down. Such chambers were not uncommon in the castles and palaces of Europe. The French *sourcière*, or mousehole, measured only 91cm² (3 sq ft) and was in use until the 19th century.

The cells were relatively luxurious when compared to the horrors of 'The Pit,' a cell deep in the foundations of the Tower of London, situated below the high-water mark of the River Thames. As the river approached high tide, rats were driven upwards into the Pit in their hundreds and prisoners faced the twice-daily ordeal of fighting off hordes of biting rodents in almost complete darkness.

Imprisonment was not limited to fellons. In 1550, the first workhouse, Bridewell in London, was set up to contain poor people who had been displaced and keep them occupied. Inmates were made to work hard for the privilege of food and shelter because houses of correction were self-financing. Typical employments included beating hemp, working treadmills, making nails or cleaning the sewers. By 1576 each every jurisdiction in England was obliged to provide a house of correction for the troublesome poor.

By the 17th century the boundary between prisons and houses of correction had become blurred. Judges began sentencing minor offenders to bridewells to relieve the chronic overcrowding in prisons. With the presence of felons, a prison regime was needed and punishments such as flogging and the stocks were employed, and not just for felons but for the poor who, after all, had committed no crime. At Bridewell a gallery was built so that a paying audience could watch the prisoners being flogged.

Newgate prison

Newgate Prison was London's most notorious prison, famous for its squalor and moral turpitude. It was originally built by order of Henry II in 1188 and from the outset was home to London's worst criminals. It held prisoners awaiting execution alongside common criminals, debtors, religious offenders, rebels, traitors, spies and those awaiting trial.

Throughout most of the 18th century, Newgate suffered from appalling overcrowding. Accommodation originally designed to hold 150 housed as many as 300 inmates, along with their families and even their pets. Robbed of their means of support, inmates' wives and families often had little choice but to accompany their husbands. Not that the prison afforded inmates' families any protection. Wives and daughters were prey to abuse and rape was common, not only by other inmates, but by the jailers too. Hunger forced some women to sell themselves for a few pennies, while women already convicted of prostitution simply continued their trade inside. When prison

IN MANY CASES, THE SPREAD OF DISEASE IN PRISONS MEANT THAT A PRISON SENTENCE OFTEN CONSTITUTED A POSTPONED DEATH SENTENCE.

LEFT: London's infamous Newgate prison stood on the same site for some 800 years. A new prison was built starting in 1770, but in 1780 it was burnt down in the anti-Catholic Gordon Riots. Newgate burnt down again in 1877, the rebuilt prison standing until 1904, when it was demolished to make way for the expanded Central Criminal Courts.

reformer Elizabeth Fry visited Newgate in 1813, she saw women who 'had been reduced to the level of wild beasts'.

Like other European prisons, Newgate was privately run. Only the most meagre rations were provided, but prisoners could buy better food, albeit at a hefty mark-up, from their jailer. Everything had to be paid for – candles, coal, even beds and bedding. Alcohol was readily available and gambling was endemic. Prisoners were even charged for temporary release from their shackles to warm themselves by the fire.

ABOVE: Reformer Elizabeth Fry at Newgate Prison, London. Fry's first visit to Newgate in 1813 shocked her so much that she devoted her life to reform. Fry returned several times, first to bring clothes for the children and later to set up a sewing room and school in the newly-segregated women's wing.

Criminals with enough money could often avoid imprisonment. At London's Fleet Prison, inmates paid the jailers for day-release, which became known as 'Fleet Liberty'. This was ultimately extended to the right to live in lodgings close by, with a payment to the jail keeper for 'loss of earnings'. This area around the prison, became known as the Liberty.

John Howard

English philanthropist and reformer John Howard (1726–90) did not write a book of theory but a firsthand report of the real conditions of every prison in the land. His report made it clear that prison conditions fell far short of the standards of a modern, enlightened society. When he was appointed High Sheriff of Bedfordshire, Howard took the trouble, in contrast to his predecessors, to visit the county jail. There, he witnessed the poor conditions as first hand: the prison was filthy, many prisoners were ill, the rules went unobserved and, most shocking of all, prisoners who had completed their sentences remained in jail because they could not pay the fees incurred during their incarceration.

Howard confronted the magistrates, who asked him to prove to them that any other county acted differently. Howard began a tour of the country, visiting every jail and prison. His book, *The State of the Prisons in England and Wales* published in 1777, was the result of his tour. It is not a book of theory, but a detailed factual survey of every prison in England and Wales, with a few simple paragraphs describing the condition of each one. The weight of evidence he amassed proved that the conditions he saw in Bedfordshire were universal.

He witnessed the full impact of disease in prisons, the most notorious of all of which was 'gaol fever', an acute form of typhoid. Howard wrote: 'From my own observations in 1771 and 1774, I was fully convinced that many more were destroyed by [gaol fever] than were put to death by all the public executions in the kingdom.' A report from Gloucestershire in 1783 confirmed Howard's assertion, estimating that three times as many prisoners died from gaol fever as were executed in that year. So deadly was the disease that in 1750, two convicts standing trial at the Old Bailey in London brought the disease into the court. The outbreak ultimately claimed the lives of over 50 people, including the entire jury, the Lord Mayor and two judges.

Howard's obsession with prisons did not end with England and Wales: he visited the Continent and reported on the prisons there. Howard found as he toured Europe that other nations were going through many of the same debates about punishment and reform. Most were further along the road to reform than England. Howard was particularly impressed by Dutch prisons, finding them 'so quiet, and most of them so clean' that he could 'hardly believe' he was in jail. He did not know 'which to admire most, the neatness and cleanliness appearing in the prisons, the industry and regular conduct of the prisoners, or the humanity and attention of the magistrates and regents'.

In unfavourably contrasting the 'ideal' Dutch prisons with the antiquated and barbaric conditions of England, Howard made reform inevitable. He campaigned for regular inspections, a clear management structure and the payment of a salary to the guards who until then had survived by stealing from or exploiting the prisoners.

Much of Howard's reforming zeal stemmed from his religious beliefs. He pushed for prisons to provide the conditions for reflection and repentance sadly lacking in outside society: order, cleanliness, solitude and silence. Circumstances were ultimately to prove Howard wrong; solitude and silence did not often lead to repentance. Howard's book had an immediate effect. In 1779, the Penitentiary Act was passed and so began a series of experiments and

'IN ALL MY EXPERIENCE OF FILTH, IGNORANCE, VICE, DEPRAVITY AND SQUALOR, I HAD NEVER SEEN ITS EQUAL. THE INMATES FOUGHT, WHINED, BEGGED ME FOR MONEY. I WAS HEART-FELT SORRY FOR THEM — BUT MY DEEPEST PITY WAS FOR THEIR POOR STARVELING BABIES, FORCED TO SLEEP WITHOUT PROPER CLOTHING ON THE BARE STONE FLOOR.'
—ELIZABETH FRY

reforms. John Howard's zeal for reform eventually proved to be his undoing: when he was invited by Russian prison reformers in 1791 to inspect the prisons there, he contracted gaol fever and died.

The Act specified that prisoners undertake 'labour of the hardest and most servile kind in which drudgery is chiefly required'. There could be no finer example of this than the treadmill. Invented by William Cubitt, the first treadmill was installed in London's Brixton Prison in 1817. Up to 40 prisoners stood side by side in what resembled a long water wheel. At Pentonville prison, also in London, prisoners on the treadmill were screened from each other according to strict penitentiary principles. Each in his individual wooden stall, prisoners worked 15 minutes on and 15 minutes off, with 15 shifts in each working day. All this futile effort was simply to turn a windmill-shaped fan on the ceiling round and round, earning the futile task the nickname of 'grinding the wind', as it was known by the prisoners.

Despite the best of intentions, the reforms brought by the 1779 Act merely created a new and particularly nasty form of mental torture, condemning criminals to a physically demanding, mind-numbingly dull and utterly solitary existence.

BELOW: This 19th century illustration shows a work room, based on the principles of the silent system – where no conversation was permitted – at a house of correction, in Tothill Fields, London.

Before the end of the 18th century, revolutions were to displace the old orders in France and America, and the United States would make prison its main method of punishment, providing a blueprint for modern penal practice.

Prison in the United States 1777–1865

In colonial America and the first years of the United States, there was no prison system; jails existed simply to house prisoners before trial. Sentences consisted of fines, whippings, public humiliation in the stocks or a cage, banishment, and, ultimately, the gallows. The primary aim of punishment was deterrence; little thought was given to reforming criminals or to investigating the causes of crime. The prevailing line of thought was very much that criminals, like the poor, will always be with us.

If the comparatively light punishments of fines, whipping or banishment failed to deter, there were few other options open to the authorities short of hanging. The Massachusetts assembly ordered in 1736 that a thief be fined or whipped on first conviction. If found guilty of a second offence, he was to pay a triple fine, sit for an hour on the gallows with a noose round his neck and then be given thirty lashes. For the third offence he was hanged.

After independence, Americans set about repudiating their colonial legacy and constructing a new and distinctly American society. High on the list of institutions ripe for reform was the colonial justice system, which mirrored Britain in mandating the death penalty for a huge array of crimes. Benjamin Rush, Pennsylvania physician and signatory of the Declaration of Independence, stated that:

Capital punishments are the natural offspring of monarchical governments … Kings consider their subjects as their property; no wonder, therefore, they shed their blood with as little emotion as men shed the blood of their sheep or cattle. But the principles of republican governments speak in a very different language.

Newly independent Americans saw the severity of colonial punishments as a major contributing factor to lawlessness. Such punishments were so severe that juries had been reluctant to commit all but the most hardened criminals to the gallows. The result was that petty criminals went unpunished and were encouraged to continue their lives of crime.

A reform movement grew up, urging the government to adopt a penal system that would embody the democratic principles of America and demonstrate the new nation's practical and moral superiority over older, less evolved forms of government. The death penalty was replaced by long-term or

CAPITAL PUNISHMENTS ARE THE NATURAL OFFSPRING OF MONARCHICAL GOVERNMENTS… KINGS CONSIDER THEIR SUBJECTS AS THEIR PROPERTY; NO WONDER, THEREFORE, THEY SHED THEIR BLOOD WITH AS LITTLE EMOTION AS MEN SHED THE BLOOD OF THEIR SHEEP OR CATTLE. BUT THE PRINCIPLES OF REPUBLICAN GOVERNMENTS SPEAK IN A VERY DIFFERENT LANGUAGE.'
—BENJAMIN RUSH

RIGHT: The penitentiary at Menard, Illinois around 1900. Strict penitentiary principles had been abandoned by this date, along with any pretensions to reform. American prisons at the turn of the 20th century were places of containment with strict regimes of order and discipline.

lifetime incarceration leading to the building of state prisons in nine states by the early 1800s. In a society built on principles of freedom, the ultimate sanction was to be the loss of liberty.

It was thought that, freed from the distorting effects of a brutal colonial penal system, the natural virtues of Americans would prevail. It was even thought that, within time, crime might be eliminated altogether. The reality was that prisons soon became unmanageable to the point where they were contributing, if anything, to lawlessness. Prisoners lived together in large rooms, abundantly supplied by alcohol and with nothing to occupy their time but planning riots, escapes and further crimes. What they lacked, reformers believed, was order; what they needed was a 'system'.

Rehabilitation

In the 1820s, under the reforming influence of President Jackson, penitentiaries were constructed to turn the offender into a law-abiding citizen. Assigned a regime based around discipline, hard labour and solitary confinement, the prisoner's time and space were minutely and completely defined. It was believed that this ordered regime would give the prisoner ample time to repent and acquire morally improving work habits.

Rival penitentiary 'systems' were introduced in New York and Pennsylvania, although there was little to distinguish between the systems except the degree of obsession with which they pursued their principles. In the New York penitentiaries at Auburn and at Ossining (better known as Sing Sing) prisoners slept alone, one to a cell. They ate and worked together, but were forbidden to speak or engage in any other form of contact.

The Pennsylvania system took the penitentiary ideal to its logical conclusion. On arrival, a prisoner's head was hooded so he would not see or be seen by anyone, and for the entire duration of his sentence, he was isolated from other prisoners and forbidden any correspondence with his friends and family. His only reading matter was The Bible; his only diversion was work to be completed in his cell, usually spinning wool.

The American prison system was not without its critics. During his 1842 tour of the United States, Charles Dickens visited the Pennsylvania prison and found it 'cruel and wrong'.

The sheer practical problems in implementing the penitentiary ideal were apparent from the outset. The most urgent and difficult problem was what to do with recalcitrant inmates who turned out to be obstinate, hardened criminals after all and not the good citizens who had simply gone bad that the penitentiary ideal had supposed. Under the cloak of reform, brutal punishment of offenders was not only tolerated but also morally

'AT SOME POINT WE MUST ASK OURSELVES: 'WHAT IS THE MORAL PRICE WE PAY FOR LOCKING UP OUR YOUTH RATHER THAN LIFTING THEM UP?' UNTIL SOMETHING IS DONE ABOUT THIS STAGGERING PRACTICE WE CAN NO LONGER CLAIM TO BE THE LAND OF THE FREE.'
—REV. JESSE JACKSON

justified. The whip was a common punishment in New York, Massachusetts and Ohio, while Pennsylvania used an iron gag and Maine employed a ball and chain.

By the 1860s and 70s, the American habit of handing down long sentences had begun and helped to create the conditions familiar to this day: rampant overcrowding and a prison population increasingly composed of the most serious criminals. Corruption and a lack of public funds exacerbated the situation, forcing the emphasis to shift simply to containment. The penitentiary experiment was over.

US PRISONS TODAY

The United States is not only the inventor of the modern prison, but also the world's leading jailer, comprising some two million people. While the US population has risen by only 20 per cent in the last 20 years, the number of

BELOW: Warden of Sing Sing prison Thomas Mott Osborn (right), posing in a cell block with two guards. Osborn attempted to relax the notoriously harsh conditions at the prison, but was accused of destroying discipline and forced to resign in 1916, after only two years as Warden.

Americans behind bars has quadrupled, at a cost to the nation of approximately $46 billion every year.

Mass incarceration has had little effect on crime rates, which have risen, fallen and risen again and are now at much the same level as in the 1970s. A study undertaken by the University of Texas revealed that in the last decade the incarceration rate in West Virginia rose by 131 per cent, but that crime fell by only 4 per cent. In neighbouring Virginia, the incarceration rate rose just 28 per cent, but crime fell by 21 per cent.

In its report 'Debt to Society', the magazine *Mother Jones* asks:

> How did this happen? How did a nation dedicated to the principles of freedom become the world's leading jailer? The answer has little to do with crime, but much to do with the perception of crime, and how that perception has been manipulated for political gain and financial profit.

Much of the blame must be laid on mandatory minimum sentences, which ensure that offenders are locked up for a set time, with no possibility of parole and without regard for any mitigating circumstances. During the 1980s, politicians outdid each other to be seen as the toughest on crime and now the federal government and virtually every state has mandatory minimum sentences. Even arch-conservative Justice William H. Rehnquist thinks these laws have more to do with politics than criminology stating that: 'Mandatory minimums are frequently the result of floor amendments to demonstrate emphatically that legislators want to "get tough on crime".'

The 'war on drugs', first declared by Richard Nixon in 1968 and pumped up in the early 1980s in response to the crack epidemic, has filled the prisons with nonviolent, predominantly black and hispanic drug offenders. New York has some of the toughest drug laws, with minimum 15-year sentences for possession of even very small amounts. There are now over 500,000 drug offenders in US prisons, a figure that is ten times larger than the 1980 figure.

'Three strikes' laws, introduced by the federal government and 23 states in the early 1990s, have swelled the prison population further. These laws, which mandate sentences of 25 years or more for third offences, have undoubtedly ensured that some violent felons are kept off the streets, but they are very much a blunt instrument. Life sentences have also been handed down for offences including possessing a stolen bicycle or stealing a spare tyre.

The costs of subsidizing such a large prison population, both economic and social, are enormous. In 1995, California, for the first time, spent more on prisons than education. It costs $5,500 to educate a youth and $20,000 to lock up a youth, so schools are losing out on funding that is being redirected

'I BELIEVE THAT VERY FEW MEN ARE CAPABLE OF ESTIMATING THE IMMENSE AMOUNT OF TORTURE AND AGONY THAT THIS DREADFUL PUNISHMENT, PROLONGED FOR YEARS, INFLICTS UPON THE SUFFERERS … I HOLD THIS SLOW AND DAILY TAMPERING WITH THE MYSTERIES OF THE BRAIN, TO BE IMMEASURABLY WORSE THAN ANY TORTURE OF THE BODY.'
—CHARLES DICKENS

CHAIN GANGS

In 1919, the state of Florida used forced prison labour to build the new highways for its burgeoning tourist industry. Chained together in work gangs, they toiled in the blazing sun all day, overseen by armed prison guards and members of the public. Those who committed infractions like 'eyeballing' — looking around instead of at their work — were beaten. More serious infractions were punished by being locked in the windowless furnace of the 'sweat box,' a wooden box measuring 2m x 2m x 1m (6ft x 6ft x 3ft).

Chain gangs were segregated according to race, by far the largest number being African-Americans. Other states followed suit and the sight of black prisoners chained together along the roadsides became a common one in the South. Prisoners were also leased out to work on private farms and plantations. A generation after the ending of slavery, black men had become slaves again.

Chain gangs continued to be used intermittently across the South, the practice only dying out in the 1950s. In recent years, some states including Alabama, Florida and Arizona have reinstated chain gangs.

towards prisons instead. As Jesse Jackson put it: 'We are increasingly becoming a nation of first-class jails and second-class schools.'

The social costs of American prison policies have fallen unequally on minorities and on young black men in particular, who in the mid-1990s formed half of the prison population and now account for about a third. Black and hispanic communities have been devastated by incarceration, losing the input and creativity of an entire generation to prison warehousing. They are also losing their democratic rights. In many states, present and former offenders lose the right to vote. More than this, prisoners are encouraged to register for the census so their 'voice can be heard'. What this means is that the prisoners swell the census counts of the largely white, rural and conservative areas where prisons are located, but have no say in choosing the policies that determine what that money is spent on.

THE STATE OF WORLD PRISONS

The human rights organization Amnesty International is currently investigating prison abuses on every continent. Amnesty has recently focused its attention on brutality in Japanese prisons, child prisoners in Burundi, political prisoners in Malaysia and the denial of visits by humanitarian observers to suspected terrorists held by the US at Guantanamo Bay in Cuba. In Brazil, riots have broken out resulting in the killing of inmates. These riots are symptomatic of long-term abuse and corruption endemic in Brazilian prisons, where overcrowding, violence and torture are widespread.

In Turkey, Amnesty International has been concerned with the recent practice of moving some 2000 political prisoners into new 'F type' prisons in which inmates are kept in isolation or small groups, denied association and visits and given only restricted access to lawyers. There have also been widespread reports of torture and beatings.

In January 2002, the Turkish Justice Minister announced that prisoners were allowed to associate for five hours a week, on the condition that the prisoners complete a vocational, educational or training programme which prisoners believe amounts to political 're-education'. More than 1000 prisoners have been on hunger strike since the opening of the first F-type prisons and over 50 have so far died.

In the UK, controversy surrounds the detainees

MARTIN LUTHER KING, JR. (1929–68)

Martin Luther King's 1963 'Letter from Birmingham City Jail' was written in response to his critics in the church who urged him to take a more moderate stance in the struggle for civil rights. King wrote the piece at lightning speed on scraps of paper and the margins of newspapers and his attorney smuggled it out. It survives as an impassioned testament to the struggle for civil rights: 'One day the South will recognize its real heroes. ... One day the South will know that when these disinherited children of God sat down at lunch counters they were in reality standing up for the best in the American dream.'

ABOVE: Edward Bunker, who played 'Mr. Blue' in the film *Reservoir Dogs*, began writing hard-boiled crime novels in prison and on his release made a new life for himself as a novelist, screenwriter and actor – specializing in playing tough guys.

at Belmarsh high security prison after reports of cruel treatment of prisoners detained under the Anti-terrorism, Crime and Security Act 2001 (ATCSA) in the aftermath of September 11. Held in small cells for 22 hours a day, the Belmarsh inmates get one hour for exercise and the another hour which is split between association with other prisoners, making telephone calls, showers and using the gym. They have inadequate health care, impeded access to legal advice, restricted contact with the outside world and limited time for religious worship.

At the time of writing, none of those detained had been charged and no information had been given on the information leading to their arrests.

Open prisons: Jyderup

While much of the world followed the American example in building ever stricter maximum-security prisons, the 20th century also saw the creation of 'minimum-security' open prisons, where the inmates may have their own room and key or even be free to leave.

Open prisons are used around the world to house low-risk minor offenders, but in Denmark they are the norm. Jyderup prison is typical of the open prisons that house 90 per cent of all convicted criminals. Jyderup attempts to re-create as far as possible the conditions in the outside world and maintains strong ties with the local community. No distinction is made between those serving short and long sentences in assigning prisoners to closed prisons. Only offenders regarded as posing a special security risk are held in closed prisons.

At Jyderup, most prisoners have their own rooms. There are no bars on the windows and prisoners can bring their own clothes and personal items, including televisions, furniture and razors. They are given an allowance to buy food, toiletries or anything else they need from the prison store. They are also paid for work or attendance at school. Facilities include a fitness room, art room and music studio, which are available to all prisoners in their free hours of 3 to 9 p.m.

Prisoners all have the right to home visits and weekend leaves of absence. In fact, there is nothing to stop them hopping over the low fence that marks the prison boundary. Not surprisingly perhaps, one in ten prisoners does just that, but the usual reason is not to escape but to avoid a conflict with another prisoner. When this happens the problem is resolved and the prisoner either returns or is transferred to another prison. Escapees who are caught by the police are returned to the prison to complete their sentences. No punitive action is taken. The only real sanction that can be imposed at Jyderup is transfer to a closed prison.

Jyderup represents an ideal of imprisonment, in which, in the words of its governor Hans Jørgen Engbo, 'the concept of punishment has been redefined to consist in nothing but the deprivation of liberty.'

BELOW: This aerial photograph shows the parimeter wall and main prison blocks of Belmarsh high security prison in southeast London.

CHAPTER SEVEN

TORTURE

Torture has been used for thousands of years, most notably in ancient Greece where it formed an essential part of the legal process. Freeborn citizens were never tortured, as it was thought that their 'noble' natures prevented them from lying. But when slaves were questioned, torture was not only permissible but mandatory; the evidence of a slave was inadmissible in an Athenian court unless he had first been tortured.

The Greek word for torture was *basanos*, after a type of slate that was used to test the purity of gold. When pure gold was rubbed against basanos, the gold left a mark that proved its purity. Similarly, a court could appeal to a freeborn citizen's honesty and intellect in telling the truth, but the testimony of a slave was held to be intrinsically untrustworthy unless 'proved' by the use of torture.

In imperial China, torture was also used judicially. The legal system required a defendant to confess to his crimes before sentence could be passed. Those found guilty but who did not confess were tortured until they did. Torture was also routinely used when interrogating witnesses during crime investigations.

The idea that the body, rather than the intellect, was the seat of truth endured in medieval Europe, where torture was regularly used in religious and civil investigations. The 'truth' was locked in the witness's body, not in his words, and it needed to be released by torture. As late as the 15th century, it was still common for a witness to be tortured while being questioned in court. A contemporary woodcut shows a prisoner strung up by his wrists being painfully stretched before the judge.

AGAINST TORTURE

The idea of truth as something impersonal, existing outside the human mind, began to disappear with the rise of the Enlightenment notion of the individual in the 18th century. After this, torture was seen merely as a means to an end,

LEFT: Water torture was a favoured method of the Inquisition. Here a woman is tied to a bench as water is poured into her mouth. The purpose-made bench has holes to allow the water to drain away.

to make the witness tell the truth that he is concealing in his mind. Torture gradually began to disappear from the courtrooms to the dungeons and back rooms where it has remained ever since.

Voltaire spoke out against torture, and Cesare Beccaria wrote in his *Essay on Crimes and Punishments* of 1764:

> No man can be judged a criminal until he be found guilty ... If guilty, he should only suffer the punishment ordained by the laws, and torture becomes useless, as his confession is unnecessary. If he be not guilty, you torture the innocent; for in the eyes of the law, every man is not guilty, whose crimes have not been proved.

In 1708, torture was declared illegal in Scotland, followed by Prussia in 1740, Denmark in 1771, Spain in 1790, France in 1798 and Russia in 1801. Official state-sponsored torture disappeared in Europe – although it certainly reappeared later in Tsarist Russia and the post-revolutionary Soviet Union, Hitler's Germany and post-war Greece, Portugal and Spain.

However, Europeans were not nearly so squeamish about the use of torture in their foreign colonies. As late as the 19th century, a long time after torture had been abolished in Europe, Englishman Sir Francis Galton, a founder of

RIGHT: Before torture was banished to secret back rooms, it was an essential part of the legal process. This 15th-century European woodcut shows a prisoner strung up and stretched as he testifies before the judge.

THE MAYA CIVILIZATION AND TORTURE

In the Maya civilization of Central America, which peaked in the 4th–8th centuries, torture was an essential part of Mayan life. Mayan priests performed an elaborate cycle of rituals and ceremonies, including torture and human sacrifice, to demonstrate piety, appease their gods and guarantee fertility and cosmic order.

Human blood was believed to nourish the gods and to be necessary for human contact with the gods. The blood of kings was especially valuable and defeated nobles and rulers were sacrificed in honour of the gods. Mayan rulers, as intermediaries between the human and the divine, had to undergo a ritual bloodletting and self-torture. They showed their devotion by sticking spines through their ears or penis, or dragging a thorn studded cord across their tongue, drawing blood that was spattered on to bark and burned at the altar, to be sent to the gods in the form of smoke.

pseudo-scientific 'race theory', recommended applying boiling water to the bodies of malingering native porters.

Today, torture is still with us, and new methods of physical and mental torture have been added to the already extensive list of cruelties. It is hard to see much difference between the zealous medieval inquisitor and the patriotic 20th-century KGB agent. With the sanction of their official ideologies of religion and science respectively, each justified brutal torture by lofty idealism. The wider aim of torture has also not changed: to instil fear. In 15th-century

Spain, Elizabethan England, the 20th-century Soviet Union and all too many countries today, fear of arbitrary arrest and torture is a powerful tool of repression. As an Inquisitor said in 1517, the main purpose of arrest, torture, trial and execution 'is not to save the soul of the accused but to achieve the public good and put fear into others'.

Torture is basically an excess of punishment. Leaving aside moral arguments about the death penalty, if execution is the legal penalty for a crime, it should be carried out with the minimum of suffering. Any additional pain is excess punishment and can be considered torture.

The UN Convention defined torture as:

> Any act by which severe pain or suffering, whether physical or mental, is intentionally inflicted on a person for such purposes as obtaining from him or a third person information or a confession, punishing him for an act he or a third person has committed, or intimidating or coercing him or a third person for any reason based on discrimination of any kind, when such pain or suffering is inflicted by or at the instigation of or with the consent or acquiescence of a public official or other person acting in an official capacity.

EARLY METHODS OF TORTURE

Bastinado

In bastinado, the victim is tied with his legs pointing upwards and is beaten on the soles of the feet. Bastinado was a judicial punishment in the past in Persia and Turkey and is still used around the world today as a method of torture. Hundreds of relatively light blows made with canes of split bamboo or other flexible material have the effect of sensitizing the soles so that each blow brings a wave of pain that penetrates the entire length of the body. It is said that imperial Chinese torturers practiced their bastinado skills by beating blocks of bean curd, without breaking the delicate skin.

Cutting and piercing

Knives, spikes and razors have always been a part of the torturer's toolkit. The fear of being cut is as effective as the torture itself. Cutting is too harmful to the body to be employed for long, especially if it is important to keep the prisoner alive. But as an added torment in an execution it is perfect.

Death of a Thousand Cuts

The imperial Chinese legend of the 'death of a thousand cuts', known in Chinese as *lingchi* ('lingering death'), is almost certainly a fanciful exaggeration. The method as told is that victims are expertly sliced and hacked

at. Ears, noses, nipples and fingers are all severed by a variety of sharp blades, prolonging the victim's torment before the executioner finally delivers the coup de grâce. It is thought that such punishments, if they existed at all, probably consisted of no more than three or four cuts.

There is evidence, however, of the Roman emperor Caligula, ordering executions along the lines of the death of a thousand cuts. According to Suetonius, Caligula ordered prisoners to be killed by multiple stab wounds, so that they could 'feel themselves die'.

Iron Maiden

A still more enduring legend is the Iron Maiden, the name for a kind of hinged hollow sarcophagus with inward-facing spikes, which is closed upon the victim placed inside. The spikes are designed to penetrate the victim's body without killing him, leaving him to die a lingering death. It is said that the Inquisition used such a device – in the shape of the Virgin Mary – to torture its prisoners.

ABOVE: This 1896 engraving shows bastinado – the beating of the soles of the feet – being carried out in Persia as an officially-sanctioned punishment. Bastinado is nowadays purely an unofficial method of torture.

RIGHT: Trial by ordeal was the principle judicial process in early medieval Europe. People believed that an innocent person would be divinely protected, as proof that he or she was telling the truth. Here, a man plunges his hand into a cauldron of boiling water.

There is no concrete evidence that the Iron Maiden was ever used, and the 'Iron Maiden of Nuremberg', discovered in the mid-19th century, is thought to be no more than an 18th-century Gothic curiosity. A document dated 1515 does, however, claim to describe the Iron Maiden in use:

> The doors shut slowly, so that the very sharp points penetrated his arms, and his legs in several places, and his belly and his chest, and his bladder at the root of his member, and his eyes, and his shoulders, and his buttocks, but not enough to kill him; and so he remained making great cry and lament for two days, after which he died.

Penetration
The most hideous penetrative torture was inflicted by the *poire d'angoisser* or pear of anguish, which used extensively in early modern Europe. This small pear-shaped metal device was inserted into the prisoner's mouth, anus or vagina. The interrogator then turned a screw on the pear, which expanded it so that its sharp-edged sections caused dreadful internal lacerations.

Burning: trial by ordeal
Trial by ordeal was a combination of judicial process and torture. It was believed that God would spare the righteous from the flames, so defendants were put to the test. Ordeals were overseen by priests and were preceded by prayers and the liberal sprinkling of holy water. The ritual was governed by the number three, symbolizing the Holy Trinity. Defendants typically carried a red-hot bar for nine feet. Others were made to walk barefoot over red-hot ploughshares (the cutting blades of a plough), or plunge their hands in boiling water. After the ordeal the wound was wrapped, left for three days and then examined. If the wound had healed, it was a sign from God that the defendant was innocent.

It might be thought that no prisoners were ever declared innocent in a trial by ordeal, but there are, in fact, numerous recorded instances of that happening. Leaving aside any genuine cases of divine intervention, it can only be attributed to the compassion, or the corruption of the officiating priest who for a high enough price would declare the wound miraculously healed.

Stretching: the rack
The rack is probably the best-known implement of torture there is. The victim was tied to a board by the wrists and ankles and two rollers are turned in opposite directions, stretching the victim's body to breaking point. The ancient Greeks used a rack during judicial torture and it was also a staple

'... THE IRON SHALL BE PLACED IN THE FIRE AND SHALL BE SPRINKLED WITH HOLY WATER, AND WHILE IT IS HEATING, HE SHALL CELEBRATE MASS ... AND STRAIGHTAWAY THE ACCUSED SHALL CARRY THE IRON TO A DISTANCE OF NINE FEET. FINALLY, HIS HAND SHALL BE COVERED UNDER SEAL FOR THREE DAYS, AND IF FESTERING BLOOD BE FOUND IN THE TRACK OF THE IRON, HE SHALL BE JUDGED GUILTY. BUT IF, HOWEVER, HE SHALL GO FORTH UNINJURED, PRAISE SHALL BE RENDERED TO GOD.'

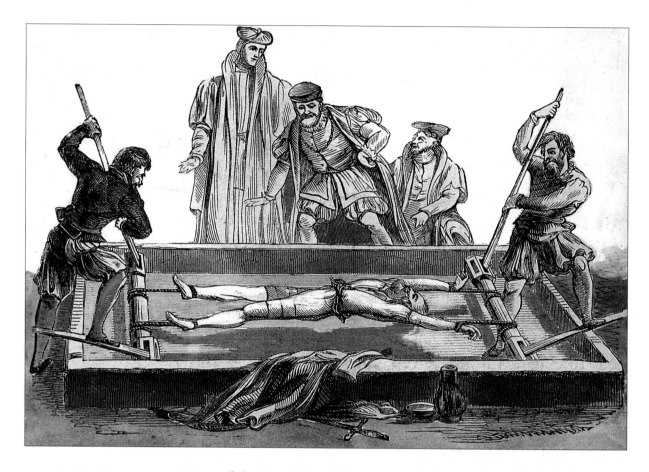

ABOVE: In this 16th-century engraving, inquisitors in Germany attempt to obtain a confession of guilt by using the rack.

torture of the Inquisition. Prisoners were also strung up by the wrists on a pulley and stretched, a torture that is still reported today.

John Coustos, an English Freemason living in Lisbon, experienced the rack after being captured by the Inquisition in 1743. Arrested as he left a coffee house and bundled into the customary waiting closed carriage, Coustos endured almost a year of captivity before he was first given a turn on the rack. He was taken to a windowless room, lit by only two candles, with padded doors to muffle the sound. He was stripped of most of his clothes and attached to the rack by iron rings around his neck and both ankles, and by a rope around each of his arms and thighs. Four men then proceeded to stretch him by pulling on the ropes until they cut through his flesh. He fainted and was returned to his cell. Six weeks later Coustos was tortured again. The entry in the Inquisition's 600-page report on Coustos states that '… he was placed on the rack and the binding commenced and he was then informed by me, the notary, that if he died during the operation, or if a limb was broken, or if he lost any of his senses, the fault would be his, and not of the Lord's Inquisitors.'

On this occasion, Coustos's arms were stretched backwards over a wooden frame, which dislocated his shoulders and caused blood to pour out of his mouth. He was stretched three times before being returned to his cell. There, surgeons reset his bones, causing him 'exquisite pain'. He was stretched a third time two months later, with the added torture of a chain around his stomach.

After this, Coustos soon gave the Inquisition details of the practices of Freemasonry and a list of its members in Lisbon. He was then told that he

LEFT: London, 1721. Highwayman Thomas Spiggott is tied to the floor of Newgate prison with 350lb (159kg) of weights bearing down on his chest. Like most defendants who refused to enter a plea at trial, Spiggott ultimately relented when 'pressed to plead'.

would be released if he converted to Catholicism, an act that he steadfastly refused to do. Coustos was held for more than a year until he was able to smuggle out a letter to the British ambassador in Lisbon, who interceded for his release. On his return to England, Coustos related his experiences in *The Sufferings of John Coustos for Freemasonry*, which was published in 1745. Coustos suffered permanent damage from his torture on the rack. He wrote:

> I have but too much Reason to fear, that I shall feel the sad Effects of this cruelty so long as I live; I being seized from time to time with thrilling Pains, with which I never was afflicted till I had the misfortune of falling into the merciless and bloody Hands of the Inquisitors.

Pressed to plead

In England, torture was illegal, yet it was common for accused criminals to be 'pressed to plead' if they refused to plead guilty or not guilty to their charge. Under English law, a defendant could not stand trial until he had pleaded the charge. The innocuous-sounding phrase 'pressed to plead' makes it sound as if the accused were urgently exhorted or possibly threatened. They were in fact literally pressed with heavy weights until they either complied or died. The torture, also known as *peine forte et dure* (strong and heavy pain), was introduced by Henry IV in about 1406 and was in use until the 18th century.

Pressing also doubled as a method of execution without the need of a trial, as recorded by London historian John Snow in 1598:

> The criminal is sent back to the prison whence he came, and there laid in some low dark room, upon the bare ground on his back, all naked, except his privy parts, his arms and legs drawn with cords fastened to several parts of the room; and then there is laid on his body, iron, stone, or lead, so much as he can bear; the next day he shall have three morsels of barley bread, without drink; and the third day shall have to drink some of the kennel water with bread. And this method is in strictness to be observed until he is dead.

In the only recorded case of the punishment in the United States, victim of the Salem witch-hunt Giles Corey refused to participate in his trial, declaring he would prefer to undergo 'what Death would put him to' rather than be found guilty of witchcraft. On 19 September 1692, Corey was pressed to death in a public square in Salem, even though the government of Massachusetts had outlawed the practice.

English law was eventually changed so that a refusal to plead was considered the equivalent to a confession of guilt. It was not until 1828 that an Act stipulated that a plea of 'not guilty' was to be entered against a prisoner refusing to plead, which remains the rule to this day.

The Scavenger's Daughter

The Scavenger's Daughter was the invention of Sir Leonard Skeffington, Lieutenant of the Tower of London during Henry VIII's reign. The device, also known as Skeffington's gyves, was a hinged iron loop in which the victim was made to kneel. It was locked and then tightened with a screw. The results of this compression of the body were horrendous, as described by the contemporary historian Matthew Tanner:

> [It] binds as in a ball, holding the body in a threefold manner, the lower legs being pressed to the thighs, the thighs into the belly and both are locked with two iron clamps … pressed against each other and the body of the victim is almost broken by this compression. … [It is] more cruel than the rack … the whole body is so bent that blood exudes from the tips of the hands and feet … the box of the chest being burst and a quantity of blood is expelled from the mouth and nostrils.

The main virtue of the Scavenger's Daughter was its convenient portability. The rack was far too big to be moved and could only be used in certain places such as the Tower of London, but the Scavenger's Daughter could be carried virtually anywhere in the kingdom. Effective in spreading terror, it accompanied torturers in the hunt for treason and heresy throughout the provinces.

ABOVE: Recorded in use from the 14th century, thumbscrews are said to have been introduced into Scotland in the mid-17th century by Thomas Dalyell, who had seen them used when serving as a general in the Russian army.

Thumbscrews

Thumbscrews consist of a split ring that encloses the victim's finger or thumb, which is then tightened by means of a wing-nut screw. Although very crude, they were easily portable and capable of inflicting terrible damage and extreme pain. More sophisticated versions held several fingers and thumbs at once, or had sharp studs inside them to increase the agony. Thumbscrews were used throughout Europe from at least the 14th century.

A simpler version of the thumbscrew used rope in place of metal rings. In Italy this was known as the *sibille*, a name coined after the Sybil of classical mythology, who guarded the Delphic Oracle, the fount of truth. In 1612, the 19-year-old Artemisia Gentileschi, before her illustrious career as a painter, accused her teacher, Agostino Tassi, of sexual assault. When it became clear during the trial that it was a question of his word against hers, Gentileschi was subjected to the *sibille* to test the truth of her claim. She secured a conviction against Tassi, who was sentenced to imprisonment, but to modern eyes it may appear that justice was secured at greater cost to the victim than the culprit.

Thumbscrews fell out of regular use in Europe during the 18th century, although, like so many other tortures, they continued to be used on colonial slave plantations.

THE KITTEE, CHEAP, PORTABLE AND EFFECTIVE, CONTRIBUTED IMMEASURABLY TO THE HEALTH OF THE BRITISH TREASURY.

The Kittee

The *kittee* was a larger Indian variant of the thumbscrew, consisting of a pair of hinged wooden boards that were brought together by means of a screw. They could be used not only on thumbs and fingers, but hands, feet, ears, noses, nipples and genitals.

Torture had been in use in precolonial India for centuries and British colonial officials eagerly kept up the tradition. The kittee was an essential piece of equipment for British tax collectors, who were permitted to use whatever means they deemed necessary to extract taxes from reluctant peasants.

Where a greater degree of persuasion was needed, two officials would use a pair of thick bamboo rods to fashion a human kittee. The victim was laid on his back across one rod, and the other was placed on his chest, legs or other parts of his body while the officials stood on either end of it.

Water: drowning

A favourite method of the Inquisition torturers, the victim was forced to drink until his belly was full to bursting point. Englishman William Lithgow was subjected to drinking by force when questioned by the Spanish Inquisition in Málaga in 1620. He endured 'a suffocating pain, in regard of my head hanging downward, and the water reingorging itself, in my throat, with a struggling

In this scene reported by a French witness in 1902, United States troops, stationed in the Philippines after the Spanish-American War, use water torture on a local official to force him to revel the location of rebel forces.

force, it strangled and swallowed up my breath from yowling and groaning.'

The torture commonly made use of a square of cloth placed over the victim's face, as described by the 17th-century Dutch chronicler Ernestus Eremundus Frisius:

The torturer throws over [the victim's] mouth and nostrils a thin cloth, so that he is scarcely able to breathe thro' them, and in the mean while a small stream

of water like a thread, not drop by drop, falls from on high, upon the mouth of the person lying in this miserable condition, and so easily sinks down the thin cloth to the bottom of his throat, so that there is no possibility of breathing, his mouth being stopped with water and his nostrils with the cloth, so that the poor wretch is in the same agony as persons ready to die, and breathing out their last. When the cloth is drawn out of his throat, as it often is, so that he may answer to the questions, it is all wet with water and blood, and is like pulling his bowels through his mouth.

A version of this treatment is used by Algerian torturers today, a grim legacy of French colonial rule. Called the torture of the *chiffon*, it involves stuffing a rag, often soaked in detergent, into the victim's mouth. Dirty water is poured though the rag until the victim's stomach is distended, then guards stamp on the victim's stomach to force the water back out through his mouth. The procedure can then start all over again.

Sleep deprivation

In the 17th century, one of 'Witchfinder General' Matthew Hopkins' favourite and most successful methods of getting innocent men and women to admit to being in league with the devil was simply sleep deprivation. Elderly parson John Lowes was 'walked', that is, marched around his cell for three days and nights without rest, until he was ready to 'confess'. Sleep deprivation was spectacularly successful in Hopkins' first case. Old widow Elizabeth Clarke was sat on a stool so high that her feet didn't touch the ground and was forced to stay awake for days. She was eventually so addled that she was quite willing to declare herself a witch and to name some 31 accomplices.

TORTURE IN THE MODERN WORLD

Torture in China is reported by Amnesty International as 'widespread', as illustrated by the case of Zhou Jiangxiong, a 30-year-old farmer from Hunan province who in 1998 was tortured to death by officials who hung him upside down, whipped him, beat him with clubs, branded him with a soldering iron and ripped off his genitals. Zhou's 'crime' was concealing the whereabouts of his wife, who was suspected of being pregnant without permission and in violation of China's strict birth control policy.

This incident is by no means an isolated case. Amnesty International's 2001 report on torture in China documents its use at all levels of society: 'Torture is widespread and systemic, committed in the full range of state institutions, from police stations to 're-education through labour' camps, as well as in people's homes, workplaces and in public.' Torture is carried out by police and other security officials, tax and fine collectors, judges, prosecutors, court clerks, party leaders and leaders of villages.

Victims of torture include political dissidents, members of the Falun Gong sect, criminal suspects and innocent bystanders. Police routinely arrest and torture those they suspect of prostitution or vagrancy. The Amnesty report describes the case of a woman who arrived on business in Guangzhou in July 1999, had her luggage stolen and was arrested by police who believed her to be a mentally ill vagrant.

She was gang-raped in a hospital for sick, disabled and mentally ill vagrants and was only released when her family paid the hospital 'treatment fees'. Although she identified her attackers and filed an official complaint, her case was stalled until it was prominently reported in the media.

In Tibet and in Xinjiang Uighur Autonomous Region (XUAR), political dissidents are routinely tortured. Amnesty reports the case of labour activist Xue Jifeng, who was arrested and confined in Xinxiang City Psychiatric Hospital from December 1999 to June 2000 and was force-fed drugs. He was released only after signing a document agreeing not to participate in politics and to stop 'caring about other people's affairs'.

Beating, burning and shaking

The simplest means of torture can be among the most effective. What need is there for anything more sophisticated than a fist, cosh or jackboot to inflict pain? Variations include tying the victim to a post, chair or bed, and leaving his body fully exposed for beating. Chilean torture victims reported being tied to an X-shaped wooden frame, with their genitals exposed for a severe beating.

Gradually, modern torturers keen to avoid the damning evidence of cuts and bruises have resorted to means other than fists and boots. Many prisoners in Pinochet's Chile disappeared and were beaten to death with impunity in the depths of Santiago Stadium, but with other prisoners the authorities were more careful. Prisoners were beaten with steel-cored rubber truncheons that left few visible marks but did excruciating damage to internal organs.

TORTURE WAS DECLARED ILLEGAL BY A UN CONVENTION OF 1984, YET THE TORTURE SURVIVORS' NETWORK ESTIMATES THAT IT IS CURRENTLY USED IN 123 COUNTRIES AROUND THE WORLD. NO GOVERNMENT WILL ADMIT TO USING TORTURE, BUT IT GOES ON, BEHIND CLOSED DOORS AND SANCTIONED BY THE STATE.

Burning

Burning is another destructive torture often used as an added torment in executions and also sometimes used as a torture in itself. Cigarettes, matches, soldering irons and boiling water are simple means of inflicting great pain. Cigarettes are a particular favourite of torturers, being cheap, readily available and capable of delivering controlled, precise pain to any chosen sensitive region of the body. Typical of many reports of torture with cigarettes are the accounts of Chilean police in the 1970s who stubbed out their cigarettes in prisoners' anuses.

Shaking

A Physicians for Human Rights report dating from 1995 gives information another method of inflicting invisible damage – shaking. The report detailed, among other incidents, the death of Abdeld El Zasmet Harizat at the hands of Israeli security forces in 1995. His autopsy recorded the cause of death as a brain haemorrhage, with no external injuries except for a few cuts and scrapes and some clear bruising where he had been grabbed by the chest. The report stated:

> In the course of his interrogation, the investigators grabbed his shirt and shook him repeatedly on several occasions. … Healthy at the time of his arrest, Harizat was brought to Haddassah Hospital in a coma after his interrogation and was certified as brain dead less than 24 hours later. …

Based on the verbal testimony of released detainees, the most common form of direct violence used by the Israeli General Security Service interrogators is not blows or kicks but violent shaking while clutching the detainee by their collars or shoulders.

Cutting and piercing

The penetration of the anus and vagina by sharp objects is another variation on the *poire d'angoisser* method described previously. In 1991, X-ray evidence confirmed a Kashmiri Arabic teacher's claim that an iron rod inserted into his anus by Indian investigators had been forced all the way through to his chest.

Insertion of needles or splinters under the fingernails and toenails is a simple and effective torture, and is one of the most ancient on record. It was the most common torture reported by Allied soldiers imprisoned in Japanese camps in World War II, and recent reports by Amnesty International recorded Chinese security forces torturing prisoners by spiking their nails and bringing their hands and feet in contact with a slow-moving electric fan.

AFTER DAYS WITHOUT SLEEP, 'WITCHFINDER-GENERAL' MATTHEW HOPKINS' VICTIMS WERE READY TO ADMIT ANYTHING. ONE ELDERLY WOMAN CONFESSED TO KEEPING IMPS NAMED ELEMANZER, PYEWACKET, PECK IN THE CROWN AND GRIZZEL GREEDIGUT, WHICH HOPKINS DECLARED TO BE 'NAMES THAT NO MORTAL COULD INVENT'.

Electric shock

A 1991 Amnesty International report outlines the case of Roberto, a 50-year-old university professor who was detained and beaten by the Zairean security forces. After a time, a senior officer arrived and immediately told the captors to stop: 'It will leave scars,' he said, 'and we will get complaints from Amnesty International.' Instead, electricity was employed as a tool of torture. For the next four weeks, Roberto's captors applied electroshock batons to the base of his spine, his genitals and other areas of his body. 'On most occasions,' the report continued, 'he vomited, lost control of his bowels and bodily functions and fell unconscious.'

Electricity is the ultimate modern torture, capable of inflicting agonizing pain and permanent damage, but without broken bones and bruises for the world's media to see. The Gestapo or Stalin's security police perhaps felt little need to conceal the beatings they administered and so did not often use

TORTURING COMMUTERS

On 31 July 1996, private security guards used stun batons to disperse passengers from an overcrowded platform at Tembisa Station in Johannesburg, South Africa. This caused a mass panic and human stampede that resulted in 16 commuters dying and 80 others incurring serious injuries. The measured tones of a government inquiry effectively summed up the incident:

The direct and most immediate cause of the disaster at Tembisa Station ... is the improper and persistent prodding and shocking of commuters with electric batons by private security guards ... the private security guards used the electric shock batons for crowd control purposes when in fact the batons are patently inappropriate for that purpose.

Although the inquiry called for the banning of such devices, so far this has not happened and South African companies continue to manufacture and export stun batons.

BELOW: The electric cattle prod, or *picana*, was first used in the stockyards of Argentina. Its power and portability were a boon to farmers, but soon proved irresistible to torturers. Before long versions were produced specifically for use on humans..

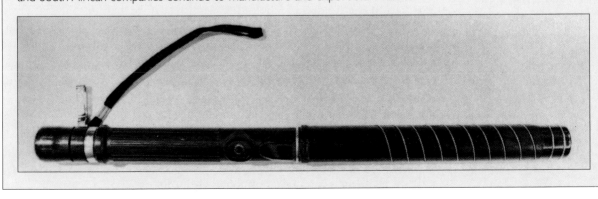

electricity. It was the French who first relied on electrical torture – out of concern for their international reputation – while fighting a dirty rearguard action in the Algerian war of independence. Frantz Fanon, author and psychiatrist, recorded cases of long-term physiological and psychological damage following electric shock torture at the hands of the French authorities in his 1961 book *The Wretched of the Earth*.

The French ran their equipment off car batteries, field telephones and other military equipment. Their usual method was to attach a fixed electrode to the victim and move the other electrode around the victim's body, genitals, mouth, hands or other sensitive areas. Security forces in the 1970s military dictatorships of South America, careful of protecting their reputations, also favoured electrical torture.

Stun batons, stun guns and stun shields

In recent years, stun batons, guns and shields, which were originally designed for use by police to subdue and arrest violent and dangerous felons, have been used to administer electric shock torture. These non-lethal electrical devices are touted as humane alternatives to guns, but all are open to abuse and have been used in documented cases of torture.

The first electrical torture device was probably the *picana* or cattle prod, developed in the Buenos Aires stockyards in the 1930s. The modern equivalent is the far more powerful electroshock baton, which is designed specifically for use against humans.

One of many cases of their use in torture is that of Mohammed Naguib Abu-Higazi, who was arrested in Egypt in 1997 under suspicion of belonging to the outlawed Islamist group al-Gama'a al-Islamiya. He was detained for nine days in an Alexandria police station, where he was blindfolded and tortured all over with an electroshock baton. Amnesty International has also reported recent electroshock baton torture in Saudi Arabia.

A stun gun is a small hand-held device with two electrodes that discharge an electric shock when they make contact with skin. A stun shield is a riot shield fitted with large electrodes that deliver a powerful shock. Former inmates at the Jackson County Correctional Facility in Marianna, Florida, USA testified to having been tortured with stun shields during 1997 and 1998:

Officers came at me with an object about 3 feet high and about 1½ feet wide, it's got wavy lines running through it, it's like a shield. ... They hit me with this twice, the first time I buckled, the second time I fell to the floor. I was hollering up a storm, screaming for help but nobody helped me.

Another detainee described being shackled to the floor while an officer repeatedly shocked him with a shield.

Stun belts

Unlike other electroshock devices, a stun belt is worn by the prisoner. The US prison system uses them as an alternative to shackling prisoners, primarily when transporting them to prison or court.

The belts are operated by remote control and can be activated by a guard standing up to 90m (295ft) away. When activated, they deliver an eight-second, high-pulse 50,000-volt shock, entering the body at electrodes placed near the kidneys. The wearer is instantly incapacitated and experiences intense pain, which rises to a peak at eight seconds. Once activated, the shock cannot be stopped.

Prisoners typically wear the belts for many hours at a time. While wearing a stun belt, a prisoner is in constant fear of severe pain being inflicted on him at any moment. He is in a state of powerlessness, completely at the mercy of the guard. As American stun belt manufacturer Stun Tech so succinctly puts it in their sales literature: 'After all, if you were wearing a contraption around your waist that by the mere push of a button in someone else's hand could make you defecate or urinate yourself, what would you do from the psychological standpoint?'

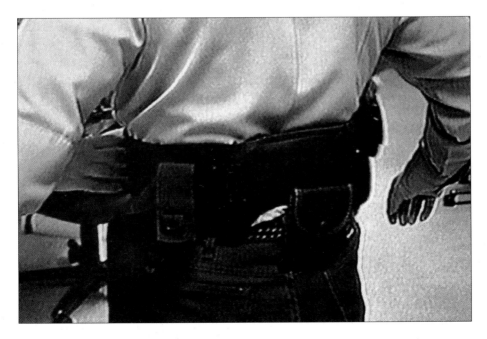

LEFT: The electric stun belt is touted as a humane alternative to shackling but in practice amounts to an instrument of torture. Prisoners wearing the belt are in constant fear of its crippling 50,000-volt shock and entirely at the mercy of the guard who operates it by remote control.

There are no official US statistics about the use of stun belts, but Stun Tech claimed in 1999 that its REACT belts had been worn by prisoners on 50,000 occasions in the previous five years. This must be a conservative estimate, as there are over 1000 belts in use in more than 100 jurisdictions.

The possibilities for abuse by unscrupulous prison officers are so great that an international campaign has been launched to ban them. Amnesty International has received several reports of guards at American maximum-security prisons using stun belts to shock, threaten and taunt non-violent prisoners.

In January 1999, Federal Judge Dean Pregerson of the Central District of California issued an injunction banning the use of stun belts in courtrooms in Los Angeles County. Pregerson noted that 'the stun belt, even if not activated, has the potential of compromising the defence. It has a chilling effect … An individual wearing a stun belt may not engage in permissible conduct because of the fear of being subjected to the pain of a 50,000-volt jolt of electricity.'

Tasers

A taser is a hand-held gun that uses compressed air to fire two darts a distance of approximately 4.5–9m (15–30ft). When the darts are embedded in the victim's skin or clothing, an incapacitating high-voltage shock is applied. Some Unites States jurisdictions have approved tasers for use by law enforcement agencies. The most celebrated use of the taser was in 1991, when a witness videotaped the arrest of 25-year-old unemployed construction worker Rodney King. King, who had committed no crime other than speeding, was twice shocked with a taser and beaten up by four officers as he lay on the ground. King received 56 truncheon blows, suffering injuries including eleven skull fractures, a broken eye socket and kidney damage. The four police officers were charged with assault with a deadly weapon and use of excessive force. On April 29, 1992, the officers were acquitted, sparking six days of rioting in which 54 people died and an estimated $700 million of property damage was done.

MENTAL TORTURE

All torture is mental torture. Inflicting pain may serve the captor's sadistic urges but pain is a means to an end, that of reaching the victim's mind. Mental torture can bypass the body and reach into the depths of the victim's psyche. In George Orwell's *1984*, prisoners in custody are taken to 'Room 101' to be confronted with their deepest fears. This is the aim of mental torture, which exists to weaken, terrify and humiliate the prisoner, to undermine his beliefs, violate his taboos, and break down his personality.

ONE OF THE MOST EFFECTIVE MEANS OF HUMILIATION IS THE VIOLATION OF SEXUAL TABOOS; AMONG THE MOST EXTREME CASES ARE THOSE OF BELGIAN POLICE OFFICERS IN COLONIAL CONGO WHO FORCED PRISONERS TO RAPE THEIR OWN MOTHERS.

LEFT: Richard Burton and John Hurt in Room 101, from the film of George Orwell's novel *1984*. In Room 101, prisoners are brought face to face with their deepest darkest personal fears, a shattering experience that breaks their resistance.

Brainwashing

Sociologist Benjamin Zablocki gives this definition of brainwashing:

> The core hypothesis is that, under certain circumstances, an individual can be subject to persuasive influences so overwhelming that they actually restructure one's core beliefs and world view and profoundly remodel one's self conception. …

Brainwashing entered the collective imagination in the Cold War, with the development of what has been called the 'Manchurian Candidate' model, named after the 1962 John Frankenheimer film of the same name. The film depicts an American serviceman who is brainwashed by the Chinese and returned to American society to lead a normal life, until triggered by a buried hypnotic suggestion to carry out a political assassination.

The 'Manchurian Candidate' model has been largely discredited, but that does not mean that brainwashing is a myth. On the contrary, numerous reports from religious, political and other groups testify to cases of suitable young people, confused, angry and vulnerable, being subjected to brutal psyche-shattering indoctrinations that prey upon their weaknesses and take them to depths of exhaustion and self-hatred, before they are 'saved' by accepting the organization's aims.

In the edition covering the end of Patty Hearst's trial, *The Saturday Evening Post* offered this definition of the typical elements in brainwashing:

1 Confinement under inhuman conditions to lower resistance.

2 The insistence on confession of past misdeeds.

3 Manipulating confessions into the context of the ideology.

4 Telling the person that his former society had turned against him.

5 'Undeserved' liberties are granted commensurate with the person's conversion, which makes the person grateful to his captors.

6 The person's weakened physical state and feeling of shame and inferiority merge into a bond with the captor.

7 Captors prove their sincerity by using the same tactics on their fellow prisoners.

8 Even upon returning to society, the person will experience confusion and doubt.

Re-education camps

Modelled on Soviet camps and staffed with guards trained by Soviet and East German agents, Vietnamese re-education camps were set up after 1975. Political opponents described by the government as 'obstinate counter-revolutionary elements' were sent to them, although often these 'opponents' were nothing more threatening than teachers, doctors or civil servants.

A prisoner's day was spent in hard physical labour and each evening in intense political indoctrination. Self-examination and confession were the essential elements of the process. Prisoners had to compile detailed 'confessions' of crimes, no matter how trivial. Confessions were written and re-written, sometimes several times a day, and any mistakes or omissions were severely punished. Prisoners were made to see their past as wrong and deserving of punishment. As one prisoner described it:

> When making declarations about relatives, we had to make mention of their guilt, as well. For example, when I stated that my grandfather had been a civil servant, I had to add that he belonged to the feudalistic social category. My father, who had been a teacher in the days of French colonization, had to be considered as having been a member of the intelligentsia, therefore a lackey of the French imperialists.

Prisoners were also made to criticize each other, which was encouraged by rewards. In the words of a former prisoner, these forums for mutual criticism were 'very effective in getting us to hate each other'.

Prisoners were constantly humiliated and in fear of physical attack. The slightest misdemeanour was punished by beatings and torture often carried out in view of other prisoners. Deaths by such beatings were common. The

'THE MORE RADICAL SORT OF PERSUASION POSITED BY THE BRAINWASHING CONJECTURE UTILIZES EXTREME STRESS AND DISORIENTATION ALONG WITH IDEOLOGICAL ENTICEMENT TO CREATE A CONVERSION EXPERIENCE THAT PERSISTS FOR SOME TIME AFTER THE STRESS AND PRESSURE HAVE BEEN REMOVED.'
—BENJAMIN ZABLOCKI

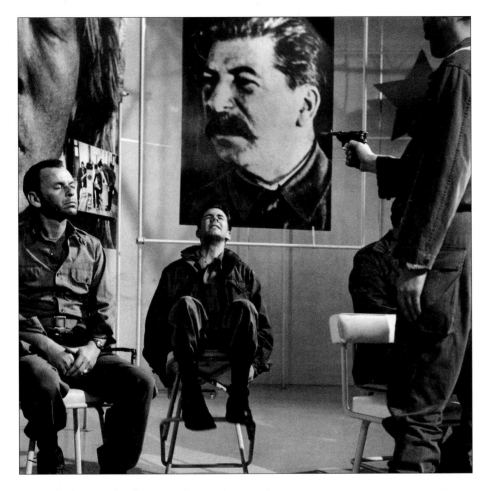

mental and physical torture suffered by the inmates led in many cases to breakdown and suicide. One former prisoner, a doctor, said he saw 'many cases – screaming, yelling people'. The doctor was forbidden by camp authorities to treat them.

Disorientation

Disorientation of the prisoner can start from the moment of arrest, preferably by surprise in the early hours of the morning, the timing calculated to produce maximum surprise and confusion. The CIA's *Human Resource Exploitation Training Manual* (obtained under the Freedom of Information Act in 1994 by reporters from the *Baltimore Sun*) states: 'When arrested at this time, most subjects experience intense feelings of shock, insecurity and psychological

ABOVE: Patty Hearst poses for the camera with gun in hand, the SLA logo drapped behind her.

HEIRESS TURNS BANKROBBER

Patty Hearst, granddaughter of American newspaper tycoon William Randolph Hearst, was a famous victim of brainwashing. At 9.40 a.m. on April 15th, 1974, four white women and a black man entered the Hibernia Bank in San Francisco. Yelling 'It's a hold-up! Down on the floor! On your faces, you motherfuckers!' the gang stole over $10,000 and fled in a getaway car. Police reviewing the security video of the hold-up were surprised to discover that one of the women was nineteen-year-old Patty Hearst, who had been kidnapped at gunpoint from her Berkeley apartment by members of radical political group the Symbionese Liberation Army (SLA) two months before. She had never been a political activist or taken up a violent cause, yet there she was on the police video, brandishing an automatic rifle and taking part in a bank raid.

When Hearst was finally captured and tried, she claimed to have been brainwashed. Hearst's defence was ineffective in cutting through the experts and counter-experts brought in to explain brainwashing to the jury, who remained unconvinced. She was found guilty and sentenced to prison, although President Carter commuted her sentence after 21 months and she was released with strict conditions of bail.

The brainwashing process as described by Hearst was a brutal regime. She was kept in isolation, repeatedly raped and beaten and told that no one would rescue her and that she would soon be killed. She was told that the privileged life she had led was utterly evil and was made to record messages of hatred towards her family and friends.

Young, sheltered and totally unprepared for the mental assault of the process, Patty Hearst was ripe material. Possibly her captors were able to build upon any feelings of guilt she may have had over her family's wealth and privilege. At any rate, she proved a model student and after two months she was ready for the Hibernia Bank raid. Hearst took part in a number of raids in the following months, carrying a loaded gun in every one. In one raid she was the getaway driver and could have easily made her escape had she wanted to. She appeared to have taken up the revolutionary cause of the SLA.

stress and have great difficulty adjusting to the situation.' The manual continues: 'Detention should be planned to enhance the subject's feelings of being cut off from anything known and reassuring.' With the victim disoriented from the start, it is easy to keep him that way by use of the 'non-coercive techniques' described in the manual.

Other methods of disorientation also include keeping prisoners hooded or blindfolded, in total darkness, in solitary confinement or even in isolation tanks, body-temperature water baths in which the prisoner floats in utter silence and complete darkness. In these conditions the mind starts to hallucinate after only a few minutes. Prisoners kept in isolation tanks for hours at a time every day can experience mind-shattering breakdowns.

Humiliation

When Turkish interrogators used cigarettes to burn the letters 'TC' (for 'Republic of Turkey') on the skin of Kurdish separatists in the 1990s, they did so to cause more than physical pain. The aim was also to humiliate the prisoner, to mock his separatist ambitions. Humiliation is an important tool of mental torture, used to underline the worthlessness of the prisoner in the eyes of the captors. Amnesty International reported in the 1980s that female prisoners in Northern Ireland were being subjected to unnecessary body

ABOVE: Suspected Al-Qaeda terrorists at the American military base at Guantanamo Bay, Cuba. As journalists and humanitarian observers are kept out, prisoners are detained without charge and without legal representation, in conditions described by witnesses and former prisoners as degrading and humiliating.

searches for no other reason than to humiliate them. The same humiliation is suffered by male and female prisoners in some of today's 'supermax' high-security prisons in the United States. Amnesty has also reported that female prisoners in Shandong province in China were strip-searched in the presence of jeering male guards.

Mental asylums

The aim of mental torture is basically to unhinge a prisoner, to make him mad. How much more effective that can be if the place of detention is a mental hospital. Starting in the Stalinist era, the Soviet Union misused its considerable expertise in the emerging field of psychology to torment those placed in mental institutions. For the most part, inmates consisted of political prisoners who opposed or criticized the government, including authors, journalists and academics.

In the perfect Socialist utopia of the Soviet Union, it was obvious that anyone who opposed the system was mad. Dissidents could be, and were, tried and punished by the civil courts, but they could also be committed to psychiatric hospitals for 'treatment', after being charged with such anti-social acts as 'mania for reconstructing society', 'reformist delusions' or 'nervous exhaustion brought on by a search for justice'. Housed among the criminally insane, inmates who arrived perfectly sane found themselves slipping into insanity. Since inmates had not been sentenced, they could remain in mental hospitals for 15, 20, even 30 years or more, until the doctors declared them 'cured' or no longer a threat to society. In many ways, the environment of a mental hospital itself does the best job of turning a sane inmate's mind. One former inmate of a Soviet hospital recalled:

> There was an everyday kind of torture which consisted of a thought, a constant image that arose from what I saw around me in the psychiatric hospital: people out of touch with their surroundings. You say to yourself: that's what I may be like tomorrow. You begin to check up on yourself every morning, looking for the first signs of madness.

Inmates in Soviet psychiatric hospitals were also turned into living vegetables by high doses of tranquillizers including chlorpromazine and insulin. As a doctor testified: 'The sedative effect is pursued to the point of stupor. This results in more or less massive disturbances in the train of thought, a positive destructuring of the mind.'

Mental hospitals also experimented on inmates with the latest psychotropic drugs such as LSD. Repeated strong doses of these drugs were

PERSISTENT MANIPULATION OF TIME; RETARDING AND ADVANCING CLOCKS; SERVING MEALS AT ODD TIMES; DISRUPTING SLEEP SCHEDULES; DISORIENTATION REGARDING DAY AND NIGHT; UNPATTERNED QUESTIONING SESSIONS; NONSENSICAL QUESTIONING; IGNORING HALFHEARTED ATTEMPTS TO COOPERATE; REWARDING NON-COOPERATION.

highly effective in breaking down an inmate's personality, bringing on severe psychotic reactions that caused long-term mental damage. Other drugs were used simply for the appalling side effects they produced. A favourite drug of the Soviet system was sulfazine, originally developed as a cure for malaria and used to treat schizophrenics in the 1920s and 1930s. Its side effects included raging fever, nausea, disorientation and intense muscle spasms.

The pain was so strong that patients could no longer stand or even sit down, but were forced to lie on their beds, relying on other inmates willing and able to do so to bring them food. The agony was relentless: Sulfazine was 'prescribed' in courses of weeks or months at a time.

A DIRTY SECRET

Torture is today's dirty little secret. Outlawed all over the world, torture is documented on every continent. It may be hidden away in a back room or a semi-official component of a corrupt system, but either way it is certain, as Beccaria pointed out almost 300 years ago, that torture plays no part in any modern definition of fair trial and just punishment.

Perhaps the best that can be said is that it is becoming harder to conceal torture from international scrutiny and the efforts of groups like Amnesty International have been successful in exposing and ending numerous instances of torture.

LEFT: A demonstrator in Vienna sports a noose around his neck as he holds up photos to protest against the death penalty imposed on Kurdish separatist leader Abdulla Ocalan. Supporters of Ocalan claim he was tortured while he was in Turkish custody.

CHAPTER EIGHT

THE DEATH PENALTY

The death penalty was first enshrined in law in the Babylonian Code of Hammurabi in the 18th century BCE, which codified 25 capital crimes. The Bible contains the first reference to divine justification for execution:

Whosoever shall shed man's blood, his blood shall be shed; for man was made to the image of God. (*The Bible*, Genesis 9:6)

The Hebrew legal code prescribed the death penalty for a wide range of offences; in Exodus 21, death is prescribed for murder, wilful assault on your father or mother, cursing a man's father or mother, and kidnapping.

The prevailing form of capital punishment among the Jews was stoning to death. The Bible's Book of Esther also tells us that hanging was the preferred method for the Assyrians, who built a gallows '50 cubits high' to hang Mardochai, a Jew.

The ancient Greeks employed the death penalty for wilful homicide and many other offences. Traitors were punished by death, their goods were confiscated and their houses razed to the ground. Executed traitors' bodies were not permitted a burial in Athens; Thucydides relates how the bones of Themistocles, who was executed for treason, were secretly smuggled into Athens by his friends so he could be buried there.

Capital offences in ancient Rome included witchcraft, poisoning or the making of poison, treason and perjury by a high official. Methods of execution included beheading, crucifixion, beating, burning and being thrown to the beasts. Those who murdered a parent or grandparent were condemned to be flogged until they bled, and then sewn up in a sack with a dog, a cock, a viper and an ape, and thrown into the sea.

LEFT: The electric chair was first used in 1890 in Auburn prison, New York and continued to be used throughout the 20th century. Its use declined in the later years of the century and it was finally declared unconstitutional in 2002.

In the Middle Ages all European countries applied capital punishment for a wide range of offences. The era is most often associated with the punishment of death by burning. For 500 years heretics and witches were burned at the stake. Canon law forbade the shedding of blood, so in cases of heresy religious courts were charged with determining the guilt of the accused before handing him over to the secular authorities for punishment.

RIGHT: Sir Walter Raleigh is beheaded in Old Palace Yard, London, in 1618 for engaging in hostilities with the Spanish, against King James's instructions to keep the peace. Beheading was an upper-class method of execution; commoners were usually hanged.

Hanging was the preferred method of execution in England before William the Conqueror banned it. William was opposed to capital punishment, although he had no qualms about beheading his political opponents, starting with the Duke of Northumberland in 1076. By the reign of Henry VIII hanging was back, along with other methods including burning, boiling and quartering. As many as 72,000 people were executed under Henry, for crimes including treason, not confessing to a crime or marrying a Jew.

The number of capital crimes in England continued to rise until, by the 18th century, a total of 222 crimes carried the death penalty, including stealing, cutting down a tree, robbing a rabbit warren and defacing Westminster Bridge. The laws were so severe that juries were reluctant to convict defendants charged with minor offences. This situation led to calls for reform and between 1823 and 1837 the death penalty was eliminated from over 100 of the 222 capital crimes.

METHODS OF EXECUTION

Burning

Burning was one of the most common execution methods used by the Romans to kill Christians. Prior to their execution, victims were often tortured by having their hands placed in hot coals or by being made to walk over them. Some Christians were bound by oil-drenched ropes and set alight, thrown into burning pits or into cauldrons of boiling oil or molten lead. Others were roasted over hot coals or even cooked alive.

According to legend, St Lawrence was killed in Rome in 258 CE by being roasted on a gridiron. When he was cooked on one side, he told his executioners that it was time to turn him over and asked if they would like a taste to see if he was better raw or cooked. Though St Lawrence was almost certainly beheaded, the tall tale persisted, earning him the ironic title of patron saint of cooks.

The historian Josephus records that the Maccabees, the Jewish rebels against Roman rule, were killed by being boiled or fried to death. Victims were thrown into boiling water, or fried in oil or tallow on a heated metal surface.

Nero is remembered as the emperor who 'fiddled while Rome burned,' or, more accurately, is reputed to have played the lyre as he watched the Great Fire of Rome devastate the city in 64 CE. Nero blamed the Christians for the blaze, despite a total lack of evidence, and lost no time in extracting his revenge. Christians were crucified, fed to packs of ravenous dogs and doused with pitch and set alight as human torches to light the Emperor's way home.

In medieval and early modern Europe, death by burning was a punishment reserved for arsonists, heretics and witches. From the 11th to the 18th

ACCORDING TO LEGEND, ST LAWRENCE WAS KILLED IN ROME IN 258 CE BY BEING ROASTED ON A GRIDIRON. WHEN HE WAS COOKED ON ONE SIDE, HE TOLD HIS EXECUTIONERS THAT IT WAS TIME TO TURN HIM OVER AND ASKED IF THEY WOULD LIKE A TASTE TO SEE IF HE WAS BETTER RAW OR COOKED.

PERILAUS'S BRAZEN BULL

BELOW: To the left, a man is cooked in Perilaus' brazen bull, while two other men suffer the rack in this scene from the Spanish Inquisition.

The Roman satirist Lucian wrote in the second century BCE of the Greek inventor Perilaus who constructed a life-size, hollow brazen bull, with an entrance at the back for victims to be placed inside. A fire was then lit under the bull's belly, cooking the victim alive. Thanks to a concealed system of pipes, the victim's screams emerged as lowing from the bull's mouth. When Perilaus presented his invention to the tyrant Phalaris, he was so impressed that he ordered Perilaus to be placed inside, declaring that he could think of no more fitting end for the inventor of such a diabolical instrument of death.

LEFT: Girolamo Savonarola was a powerful Florentine cleric who preached against the luxury and excess of the Church. The Pope had him arrested and tortured in 1498, before handing him and two accomplices over to the civil authorities to be hanged and burned.

centuries, at least 200,000 people died at the stake. Heretics were burned at the hands of the Inquisition of Rome and the later Spanish Inquisition. In England, both Catholics and Protestants were burned at various times, and witches were fanatically hunted down and burned in England, Germany and throughout the rest of Europe.

ABOVE: An *auto-da-fé* in the courtyard of the Spanish Inquisition in Lisbon, Portugal. Each victim wears a high cap of card and a tunic painted with the flames and cruel devils of Hell. Priests stand nearby, ready to receive a confession of guilt even as the victims wait to be burned.

The auto-da-fé

In 1479, Ferdinand and Isabella united the kingdoms of Castile and Aragón, and when their capture of Granada in 1492 finally ended Moorish power, they set about unifying Spain under Catholic rule.

In 1478, Ferdinand and Isabella asked permission of the Pope to begin a Spanish Inquisition to 'purify' the people of Spain and drive out those opposed to Catholicism – Muslims, Jews and *conversos*, those who claimed to have converted to Catholicism but who continued to practice their original religion in secret.

Mass trials of heretics were conducted, and the guilty were burned together in a ceremony known with grim irony as an *auto-da-fé* (act of faith). The first *auto-da-fé* was held on 12 February 1481 in Seville, when six men and six women were burned alive for practicing Judaism.

The long, spectacular ceremonies combined execution, religious service, theatre and propaganda and were usually held on public holidays to maximize the number of spectators. The grand finale was the sight of the burning pyres lighting up the night sky, on raised platforms so that they could be seen by all. Not all of the victims were burned alive; in some cases those executed by other means were burned in effigy. Others, convicted posthumously, were dug up and burned.

On 30 June 1680 in Madrid, 51 people were burned alive or in effigy in a 14-hour *auto-da-fé* held to commemorate the marriage of Carlos II to Louis Marie d'Orléans. The king himself set light to the first pyre. Carlos II's successor, Philip V, later refused the same 'honour' when an *auto-da-fé* was held to honour his own wedding. The last *auto-da-fé* was held in 1790.

BURNING CATHOLICS AND PROTESTANTS

In a five-year period, first Catholics, then Protestants, then again Catholics were burned at the stake in Eng;and. After Henry VIII broke with Rome, he had Catholics burned as heretics. His daughter Mary (r. 1553–58) came to the throne after the death of her brother Edward VI. A devout Catholic, Mary married Philip II of Spain and embarked on a series of religious persecutions of Protestants. During her brief five-year reign she burned some 300 Protestants, including rich and poor men, women and even children, earning her the name 'Bloody Mary'. Mary died childless and the throne passed to her Protestant sister, Elizabeth I, when Catholics were burned once again.

The Spanish Inquisition's jurisdiction extended to Spain's American territories. On 11 April 1649, the largest *auto-da-fé* in the New World was held in Mexico. All but one of the 109 victims was burned under accusation of practicing Judaism. Thirteen were burned alive and 57 in effigy. Of the 13, 12 'repented' and so were garroted before being burned.

When the Pope issued a Papal bull in 1484 confirming the existence of witchcraft, it sparked off witch-hunts throughout Europe. He gave two of his inquisitors, Heinrich Kramer and Johann Sprenger, authority to investigate charges of witchcraft. Two years later they published a 500-page manual on the subject named *Malleus Maleficarum*. This spread the doctrine beyond the reach of the Spanish Inquisition and within 30 years of its publication it had been adopted by the Protestant churches of northern Europe. By the end of the 16th century, Catholics and Protestants alike were burning witches in their hundreds.

Between 1587 and 1593, the Archbishop-Elector of Trèves burned 368 witches, an average of more than one a week. The Prince-Bishop of Bamberg burned over 600 witches between 1623 and 1633 and the Prince-Bishop of Würzburg burned 900, including 19 priests, one of his own nephews and a number of children accused of having sex with demons. None of these figures can compete with the Inquisition, which boasted of having killed some 30,000 witches over a period of 150 years.

THE WITCHFINDER GENERAL

England's Matthew Hopkins (pictured), the self-styled 'Witchfinder General', began his notorious career in 1644 in Manningtree in Essex. Motivated by a reward of 20 shillings for every witch put to death, Hopkins was scrupulous in his search, hunting out 400 witches in the eastern counties in just 14 months. Sixty-eight witches were hanged in the town of Bury St. Edmunds alone, and 19 were hanged in a single day in Chelmsford.

Hopkins' favoured interrogation techniques included ducking – if the suspect sank she was innocent, if she floated then she was guilty and was hanged. Prisoners were also stripped and examined for the 'devil's mark' and for boils and tumours, which were said to be nipples for suckling demons who had taken animal form. Some women were condemned merely for keeping pets, which they were persuaded to admit were imps or demons.

Towards the end of Hopkins' reign of terror people began to question his motives and Hopkins returned to obscurity in Manningtree as quickly as he had risen. Some speculated that he was hanged for witchcraft, but it is thought he died in his bed of tuberculosis.

It was a long time before rational thought displaced such beliefs – the last witch-burning in England took place in 1684, and the last one in Germany took place almost a hundred years later.

Crucifixion

Crucifixion was first used by the Phoenicians in about 1000 BCE. It was later imported by the Greeks, Assyrians, Egyptians, Persians and Romans, and was also used in Japan.

The Phoenicians simply nailed the victim to a stake, but a crossbeam to support the arms was later added. Other crosses were X-shaped; this shape became known as a St Andrew's cross after the saint who was reputedly crucified on one.

The crucifixion of Christ as related in The Bible accords with historical reports of the procedure. The condemned was first flogged, then made to carry the crossbeam to the site of execution. He was nailed to the cross through his palms and insteps, or else tied to it by the wrists and ankles. The cross was placed into a fixing in the ground and the victim was left to die a slow, lingering death. Often the victim would be beaten, pierced or humiliated by officials or spectators. The victim's feet rested on a wedge of wood to prevent him from falling off, and for someone of strong constitution, death could take several days.

Compassionate officials would sometimes put victims out of their misery at the end of the first day. Victims were occasionally crucified upside down, which was a mercy for the victim as it quickly brought unconsciousness. After death, the victim was left on the cross as an example and then the cross was customarily buried along with the victim.

Certainly by the time of Christ's crucifixion, crucifixion was considered a particularly humiliating form of death, reserved for slaves and the worst criminals.

The guillotine

The symbol of the bloody excesses of the French Revolution, the guillotine was conceived with the noblest of intentions. Dr Joseph Guillotin's aim in inventing the device that bears his name was to perfect a method of execution that could dispatch its victims without causing them undue suffering.

The guillotine was a perfect Revolutionary device, both efficient and egalitarian. No longer was there to be beheading for the rich, hanging for the poor, and the agonies of death on the wheel for religious offenders. With the guillotine, everyone could die like a noble. On 3 May 1791 the Constituent Assembly made it law that everyone sentenced to death was to be beheaded.

There is evidence that a device very similar to a guillotine was used by the Romans to execute St Matthew. A heavy axe-head was set into grooves running along two upright posts. The executioner then gave the axe-head a mighty whack with a mallet and the blade was propelled at high speed on to St Matthew's neck. The Persians are also believed to have used a similar device with a cross-beam and a weighted blade in the 10th century.

The immediate ancestor of the guillotine was the Halifax gibbet. This crude execution device stood in a public square in Halifax, England and was

ABOVE: Paris, 21 January 1793: the executioner holds aloft the severed head of Madame la Guillotine's most famous victim, King Louis XVI. As he did so there was a stunned silence, before the crowd erupted with cries of 'Vive la République!'

THE GUILLOTINE WAS
PAINTED BLOOD RED IN
ANTICIPATION OF ITS
FIRST EXECUTION.

SANSON, THE RELUCTANT EXECUTIONER

Six generations of the Sanson family held the post of executioner in Paris from 1688 to 1889. Charles-Henri Sanson, a lover of music, fine clothes and society parties, took over the post in 1788, one year before the Revolution.

At the peak of the Terror, Sanson executed 300 men and women in three days, and on another occasion is reported to have severed 22 heads in 36 minutes. The working conditions were appalling. Blood soaked the scaffold and gathered in a stinking pond under it. The conditions were so slippery underfoot that in 1792, Sanson's son Gabriel fell off the scaffold, sustaining injuries that were ultimately fatal.

Sanson carried out the unwavering ritual of the guillotining thousands of times, on each occasion reaching into the basket to pluck out the severed head and show it to the crowd. Taking no joy in killing, Sanson felt for the suffering of his victims and was particularly distressed when executing women. No doubt what spurred him on was the knowledge that if he shirked his duty his head would be the next on the block.

in use from 1286 until 1650. Parish records show that between 20 March 1541 and 30 April 1650, the gibbet executed 49 victims. The Halifax gibbet consisted of a pair of upright posts almost five metres (five yards) in length. Between them there was a blade, 25cm (10 inches) long and weighing 3.5kg (7lb 12oz), set in a block of wood. When the pin holding it in place was released, the heavy blade came crashing down on the neck of the victim lying below, severing his head with some force.

The gibbet was chiefly used to execute thieves. Those found guilty of stealing goods worth more than 13½ pence were to be taken to the gibbet for execution on the next market day. As a crowd gathered to watch, the men nearby assisted in tugging the rope attached to the pin that held the blade in place. In this way, the people assumed collective responsibility for taking a man's life.

Once the law requiring all those sentenced to death to be beheaded was passed, Guillotin took advice on the best way of achieving this. The executioner Charles-Henri Sanson told Guillotin that the sword would be too slow for multiple executions, as it would have to be reground after every stroke. Another adviser, Dr Louis of the French Academy of Surgery, recommended a device similar to the Halifax gibbet. Guillotin investigated the Halifax gibbet and then commissioned a German carpenter to make an improved version of the device. It was originally nicknamed the Louisette in honour of Dr Louis.

The guillotine was made up of two six-inch thick upright posts 3 metres (10 feet) in height and 60cm (two feet) apart. Unlike the Halifax gibbet, the guillotine's blade was held in place by runners, and was also weighted by a 30kg (65lb) iron weight. Another improvement was the bascule, the piece of wood to which the victim was tied. He or she was tied to the bascule while standing up and then laid down and secured under the guillotine. There was no possibility of the victim moving so that the blade missed its target – a common occurrence in beheadings by the sword or axe.

Sanson tested the new machine on corpses and live animals and declared himself pleased with the results. The first of the thousands of victims of the guillotine was Jacques Pelletier, a highwayman, who was executed on 25 April 1792 in the Place de Grève in Paris. The execution was swiftly and efficiently carried, much to the dismay of the crowd, which was disappointed by the poor spectacle, chanting: 'Bring me back my wooden gallows!'

More dramatic was the execution of France's last king, Louis XVI in 1793. Fearing arrest, the king had fled Paris, but was caught at Varennes and brought back to the capital to meet his fate. On 21 January, the king was taken to his place of execution in a carriage, guarded by troops fearful both of the angry

LOUIS XVI CLIMBED THE SCAFFOLDING, DECLARING: 'I DIE INNOCENT OF ALL THE CRIMES LAID TO MY CHARGE. I PARDON THOSE WHO HAVE OCCASIONED MY DEATH AND I PRAY TO GOD THAT THE BLOOD YOU ARE GOING TO SHED MAY NEVER BE VISITED ON FRANCE.'

revolutionary crowds and of a last-minute rescue attempt by royalists.

The journey through the streets of Paris took almost two hours. In the Place de Louis XV, guards held back a large crowd armed with pikes and other weapons. As the king left his carriage, three guards approached to disrobe the king, but he insisted on taking off his cloak and unbuttoning his shirt himself. Then, as the guards approached him to tie his hands, the king refused, saying: 'No! I shall never consent to that. Do what you have been ordered to do but you shall never bind me.' The king mounted the steps to the guillotine declaring: 'I die innocent of all the crimes laid to my charge. I pardon those who have occasioned my death and I pray to God that the blood you are going to shed may never be visited on France.'

Hanging

In Anglo-Saxon England, hanging was the official means of capital punishment and purpose-built gallows were erected as early as the fifth century. The method was simple; the noose was placed around the victim's neck and he was made to climb up a ladder that was then pulled away to leave him hanging. Without much of a drop, the victim's neck would usually not break and strangulation was the most common cause of death.

ABOVE: Here, a gallows stands outside an old-fashioned American courthouse, a reminder of how recently this style of punishment was practised in the United States.

The procedure did not change until the 17th century, when victims were driven up to the gallows in a cart, the noose placed round their necks and the horse driven away. More of a cosmetic change, this method again used a short drop that could not ensure a quick death. More significant was the addition of the hangman's knot – a knot on the noose that helped to break the neck.

In 1760, a vertical drop was used for the first time at the hanging of the Earl of Ferrers for murder. Instead of using a ladder or cart, a trap-door was opened under the victim, so that he fell until the rope jerked him to a stop, thereby breaking his neck. A fine idea, but the executioners had miscalculated. The Earl was left hanging with his toes just touching the ground, and his executioners had to pull on his legs to ensure his death.

When new gallows were built outside Newgate jail in 1783, they included a raised platform and trap-door. It was a more effective method than a ladder or cart, but the drop was still not long enough to ensure an instantaneous death in all cases. In the following decades, the authorities in Ireland started experimenting with the 'long drop'. Death was instantaneous, but the pull on the rope was so strong that the victim was often decapitated.

It was not until the next century that the 'science' of hanging was perfected. Executioner Thomas Marwood hanged his first victim in 1871 in Lincoln and is reputed to have wished all his victims a speedy death. Marwood was dedicated to the task of perfecting a humane and reliable method of hanging. He calculated the length of rope needed, taking into account the victim's weight and the muscular strength of his neck. He also found that a metal ring

BELOW: Guy Fawkes and his Catholic co-conspirators, who had attempted to blow up Parliament in the 'Gunpowder Plot' of 1605, are dragged through the streets of London on lengths of fencing on the way to the gallows.

on the noose was more effective than a hangman's knot. Marwood concluded that a drop of eight feet was effective in quickly dispatching the victim, but not so long as to decapitate him. Philanthropic campaigners took up the cause of the drop, which was soon adopted.

Hanging, drawing and quartering

This was the ultimate punishment in English law for men who had been convicted of high treason. Women were burned at the stake instead, for the sake of decency.

The condemned was tied to a hurdle and drawn by a horse through the streets to the place of execution. Once there the prisoner was hanged and then cut down whilst still conscious. His penis and testicles were cut off, his stomach was slit open and his intestines removed and burned before him, his other organs were torn out and finally his head was cut off and his body divided into four quarters. The head and quarters were parboiled to preserve them and then publicly displayed as a grim warning to all.

In 1283 David, Prince of Wales was tried for treason at Shrewsbury and was sentenced:

> to be drawn to the gallows as a traitor to the King who made him a Knight, to be hanged as the murderer of the gentleman taken in the Castle of Hawarden, to have his limbs burnt because he had profaned by assassination the solemnity of Christ's passion and to have his quarters dispersed through the country because he had in different places compassed the death of his lord the king.

In the 16th century a total of 105 Catholic martyrs were hung, drawn and quartered at Tyburn, and in 1606 Guy Fawkes and his fellow 'Gunpowder Plot' conspirators were condemned to the same fate. Fawkes was executed in Old Palace Yard in front of the Houses of Parliament and his head and those of his co-conspirators placed upon spikes on London Bridge.

Hanging, drawing and quartering remained the lawful punishment for treason until it was abolished in 1814.

Poison

Poison was the usual method of execution for Athenian freemen. Condemned prisoners were forced to drink a cup of hemlock or other poison. A far nastier death awaited condemned prisoners of low social grade, including slaves: they were beaten to death with cudgels instead.

The philosopher Socrates was condemned to death for opposing the gods and corrupting the youth in 399 BCE.

THE HALIFAX GIBBET SEVERED THE HEAD WITH SUCH FORCE THAT IT OFTEN FLEW INTO THE CROWD. ONE TALE TELLS OF A WOMAN RIDING A HORSE ALONG GIBBET STREET WHO SUDDENLY FOUND HERSELF STARING INTO THE EYES OF A NEWLY DETATCHED HEAD THAT LANDED IN HER SADDLEBAG.

RIGHT: This 19th-century illustration of an execution by the Inquisition shows how torture was often a component in executions. The victim's right hand has been cut off, before she is clubbed to death, as a priest looks on and prays for her.

The indictment stated:

This indictment and affidavit is sworn out by Meletus: Socrates the son of Sophroniscus of Alopece is guilty of refusing to acknowledge the gods recognised by the State and of introducing new and different gods. He is also guilty of corrupting the youth. The penalty demanded is death.

In Athenian trials, the procedure was that the prosecutor proposed a penalty, and then the accused had the right to propose an alternative punishment. Socrates took the opportunity to suggest that he be kept at public expense in palatial accommodation for the rest of his life. Nevertheless, the court handed down a sentence of death and Socrates drained his hemlock, spurning offers from his friends and supporters to help him escape into exile.

The wheel

A popular method of execution in medieval France and Germany, the wheel was usually reserved for those convicted of crimes against religion. The condemned was taken to a scaffold and stripped as for a crucifixion. He was then strapped across the spokes of a wheel and beaten with an iron bar until all his bones were broken.

The wheel was then propped upright so that the crowd could witness the victim's death throes. Skillful executioners could break a victim's bones without puncturing the skin to prolong his agony. Alternatively, the executioner might increase the victim's torment by placing the wheel over a fire or a bed of nails. When the executioner was ready to put the victim out of his misery, he did so with a few well-aimed blows to the chest.

PUBLIC EXECUTIONS

Prisoners were executed publicly in England, and the biggest crowds were at Tyburn, London's main execution site, which was situated at the western end of Oxford Street near what is now Marble Arch. Prisoners were led in a procession from Newgate prison to Tyburn, all the way surrounded by a rowdy, drunken crowd. The journey sometimes took as long as two hours, which included official stopping points for drinks. So

---

THE BLACK ACTS

In 18th-century England, Parliament protected property more than human life. Someone found guilty of attempted murder might be treated leniently by the courts, but someone who was guilty of forgery, poaching, burning down a hayrick or even cutting down an ornamental shrub would be put to death. The already huge number of capital offences rose still further with the passing of the Waltham Black Act of 1723, which, among other new capital offences, punished appearing on the highway with a sooty face with death.

The sheer excesses of the Act were, in fact, responsible for the push to reduce the crimes punishable by death. Judges, juries and even victims looked for any excuse to find the accused not guilty rather than to see them hanged for a trifling offence.

popular were executions that a grandstand was built in 1724 offering ringside seats at premium prices. When Earl Ferrer was hanged in 1760 the takings that day were over £5000.

In 1763, the public procession to Tyburn was ended and prisoners were executed at the newly built gallows at Newgate. Samuel Johnson publicly lamented this change, believing that public executions had a strong deterrent force and should be seen by as many people as possible.

French executions were held publicly by law well into the twentieth century. On 25 February 1922, crowds at Versailles witnessed the death by guillotine of the multiple murderer Henri Landru, known as 'Bluebeard'.

Henri Desire Landru had wooed rich middle-aged women with personal ads in newspapers. One read: 'Widower, with two children, aged 43, possessing comfortable income, affectionate, serious and moving in good society, desires to meet widow of similar status, with a view to matrimony.'

Widow Jeanne Cuchet answered the first advertisement, placed in 1915. She was bowled over by the charming Landru, who was immaculately dressed and cut a distinctive figure with a full flame-red beard. Once Mme Cuchet

ABOVE: Henri Desire Landru, known as 'Bluebeard', was guillotined outside Versailles prison in 1922 for the murder of at least eleven victims. Police found 290 fragments of bone and teeth in the furnace of his house.

had signed over her possessions to Landru, he murdered her and her 17-year-old son, burning their bodies in the house fire. He murdered two more women that year, before installing himself in the Villa Ermitage in Gambais, where he murdered seven more.

When suspicions about the new resident and his stream of lady friends began to be aroused, the mayor ordered an investigation. Police examined Landru's house and found 290 fragments of bones and teeth in the stove and numerous personal possessions spread around the house. The exact number of his victims was never fully established, and Landru never made a confession. However, he was tried and found guilty, and sentenced to death.

French executions stipulated that the execution was to be carried out in public, in front of the jail where the condemned was being held. When, late on 24 February, the news spread that Landru's final appeal for clemency had been turned down, a large crowd of journalists and onlookers descended on Versailles prison where Landru was held. The authorities, anxious to avoid a riot, began to construct the scaffold before it was light in the hope of executing Landru before the crowd got too unruly.

The executioner, Anatole Deibler, arrived at the jail at 4 a.m. and at 5.45 a.m. the guards came for Landru. Refusing the customary rum and cigarette offered to those about to die, Landru asked to be shaved and then spent several minutes with the chaplain. The prison gates opened and Landru was led towards the guillotine, barefoot, with his hands tied behind his back and wearing a shirt with the neck cut out. A small invited audience looked on, while a ring of guards kept the clamouring crowd away from the guillotine.

Landru was tied to the bascule, placed under the guillotine and promptly beheaded. Both parts of his body were then put in a horse-drawn van and driven away at a gallop. One observer who timed the proceedings reported that Landru died just 26 seconds after first emerging through the prison gates.

ABOVE: Double murderer Gary Gilmore was executed by firing squad on January 17, 1977, ending a 10-year US death penalty moratorium. Gilmore, a firm believer in the death penalty, refused to appeal his sentence and famously donated his eyes for transplant.

MODERN METHODS OF EXECUTION
Electrocution
The electric chair was first used in Auburn Prison, New York, on 6 August, 1890 on wife-killer William Kemmler of Buffalo. The chair's first victim was very nearly its last. The initial 1,300-volt charge singed Kemmler's flesh, but after 17 seconds he was still alive and it took another 70-second shock to end his life. The assembled witnesses were horrified by the spectacle and nauseated by the stench, but the design was duly improved and the device affectionately known as 'Sparky', 'Old Smokey' or the 'Hot Squat' has been in service ever since.

By the last years of the 20th century the electric chair had in most states been supplanted by lethal injection, considered to be more humane. The electric chair is now used in only 10 states and, as of 2003, Nebraska is the only state that requires electrocution. The design of the chair and the method of execution have changed little, if at all, in the past 100 years. The chair is always made of wood, usually oak. The victim is secured by straps around his arms, head, legs and chest. His head and right leg have previously been shaved where the two electrodes, moistened with saline solution, are fitted. The executioner, sitting behind the chair, administers the first shock of 2,000 volts, followed by two lesser shocks and then another 2,000-volt blast.

It is claimed that the victim dies instantly when the first shock is applied but this is not always true. One victim needed five shocks and took an agonising 17 minutes to die. Other reports speak of six-inch flames shooting out when the current was switched on.

Lethal injection

Lethal injection is unique to the United States. It was introduced in 1977 in Oklahoma and Texas and is currently the favoured method of execution in 37 states. The rise of lethal injection in the United States has all but put an end to the electric chair.

A combination of drugs is injected, and though the composition of the lethal cocktail varies from state to state, the intent is always to render the victim unconscious, then to paralyse his muscles and induce heart failure.

Problems arise when the victim has been an intravenous drug user or for any other reason has scarred or collapsed veins. If the prisoner struggles or the executioner slips, the lethal dose can be injected into a muscle, causing great pain. At other times the lethal dose coagulates and blocks the tubes, prolonging the agony. Amnesty International and other humanitarian observers have logged execution times at well over an hour with the dose having to be re-administered several times.

Lethal injection may be far from perfect but a bungled injection is a lot less messy than a bungled electrocution. In the face of constant opposition to the death penalty, the pro-execution lobby are as aware of the value of good PR as any pressure group and have worked hard to promote the myth of lethal injection as a painless, virtually automatic means of execution.

Shooting

Shooting is by far the most common method of execution in the world today. In 2001 an estimated 2500 people were executed by shooting, the vast majority in China where it is the favoured

EXECUTIONER PIERREPOINT

'I operated, on behalf of the State, what I am convinced was the most humane and the most dignified method of meting out death to a delinquent – however justified or unjustified the allotment of death may be – and on behalf of humanity I trained other nations to adopt the British system of execution … The fruit of my experience has this bitter after-taste; that I do not now believe that any one of the hundreds of executions I carried out has in any way acted against a deterrent against future murder. Capital punishment, in my view, achieved nothing except revenge.

—*Albert Pierrepoint, British hangman until his resignation in 1956, from his biography,* Executioner Pierrepoint.

method. Shooting is a lawful method of execution in 70 countries and is the sole method in 42 of them. In some cases, for example in Egypt, shooting is reserved for members of the military.

Firing squads are not often used today. In China executions are carried out by a single close-range shot to the back of the head. In Thailand, prisoners are shot by a single executioner who aims his stand-mounted machine gun at the prisoner's heart.

Utah is the only US state to have used a firing squad in recent times. On 17 January 1977, Gary Gilmore became the first person to be executed in the US for 10 years, after fighting a long campaign to be allowed to die. Under Utah law at the time, condemned prisoners were given the choice of firing squad or hanging, and Gilmore elected to be shot. On the day of execution Gilmore was

BELOW: Two men convicted of raping and murdering a four-year-old girl are executed by firing squad in Guatemala in September 1996. They were the first men to be administered the death penalty in 13 years in Guatemala.

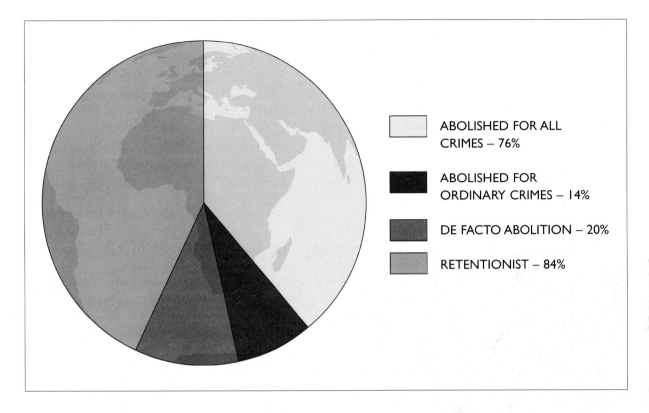

- ABOLISHED FOR ALL CRIMES – 76%
- ABOLISHED FOR ORDINARY CRIMES – 14%
- DE FACTO ABOLITION – 20%
- RETENTIONIST – 84%

tied to a chair and a white target placed over his heart. Before execution he was asked if he had anything to say and he uttered his last words, 'Let's do it.' A squad of six volunteers aimed their rifles at his heart; one rifle was loaded with blanks so that the squad members would not know whether they had fired the fatal shot.

ABOVE: More than half the countries in the world have now abolished the death penalty in law or practice.

LIMITING CAPITAL PUNISHMENT

Opposition to the death penalty began in the 18th century when, among others, Voltaire, Montesqieu and Beccaria criticized it in their writings.

> The execution of a criminal is to the multitude a spectacle which in some excites compassion mixed with indignation. These sentiments occupy the mind much more than that salutary terror which the laws endeavour to inspire. … The punishment of death is pernicious to society, from the example of barbarity it affords. If the passions, or the necessity of war, have taught men to shed the blood of their fellow creatures, the laws, which are intended to moderate the ferocity of mankind, should not increase it by examples of

barbarity, the more horrible as this punishment is usually attended with formal pageantry. Is it not absurd, that the laws, which detest and punish homicide, should, in order to prevent murder, publicly commit murder themselves?

BELOW: Executions in the United States over the past four centuries. The chart highlights the gradual rise of capital punishment in the 17th, 18th, and 19th centuries, rising to a peak of nearly 200 executions per year in the mid-1930s; a subsequent decline then a moratorium on executions between 1967 and 1977; and finally, a trend toward more executions in recent years.

In the aftermath of World War II, in 1948 the United Nations adopted the Universal Declaration of Human Rights which proclaimed the universal 'right to life' as an absolute, although it stopped short of explicitly attempting to outlaw capital punishment.

Western European nations one by one stopped using the death penalty, even if they did not technically abolish it. By the 1980s, de facto abolition was the norm in western Europe.

The death penalty today

According to Amnesty International, in 2001 at least 3048 prisoners were executed in 31 countries and at least 5265 people were sentenced to death in 68 countries. These figures include only confirmed cases; the true figures are certainly higher. In 2001, 90 per cent of all known executions took place in China, Iran, Saudi Arabia and the United States.

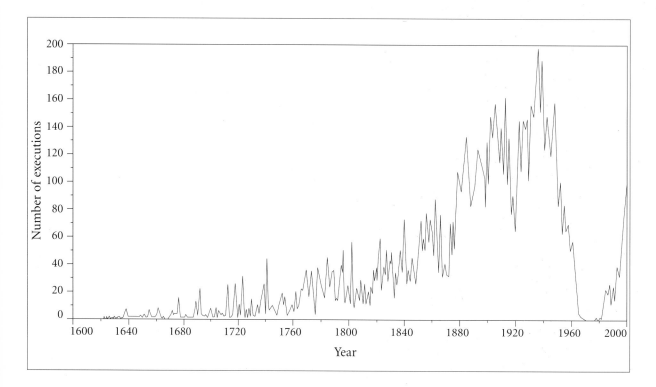

China executes more people than any other country on earth. According to Amnesty International's figures, China sentenced at least 4015 people to death in 2001 and carried out at least 2468 executions. The actual figures are thought to be much higher, but·the Chinese government does not release official counts of executions, believing such statistics to be a state secret. In April 2001, the Chinese government announced the latest of its 'strike hard' anti-crime campaigns. Between April and July 2001, at least 1781 people were executed, a figure that exceeds the number of known executions in the rest of the world combined during the previous three years. In June 2001, on World Anti-Drug Day, over 50 people were convicted of drug crimes at mass sentencing rallies and were executed. Amnesty International believes that China's 'strike hard' campaigns have led to an increase in the use of torture and introduced speeded-up judicial procedures that have resulted in numerous miscarriages of justice.

The death penalty in the United States

The first recorded execution in the American colonies was that of Captain George Kendall who was executed in the Jamestown colony of Virginia in 1608 for the crime of spying for Spain. In 1612, Virginia's governor Sir Thomas Dale

ABOVE: Public execution: a huge crowd turns out for the execution of a black man for the robbery and murder of a 70-year-old white woman in Owen's Borrow, Kentucky in 1936.

enacted the 'Divine, Moral and Martial Laws', mandating the death penalty for offences such as stealing grapes, killing chickens and trading with Indians. The New York Colony instituted the 'Duke's Laws' of 1665 which punished by death such offences as striking one's parents or denying the 'true God'.

There was a burgeoning abolitionist movement even in colonial times, particularly after the publication of Beccaria's *On Crimes and Punishment* in 1767. The first attempt to restrict the death penalty was a bill introduced by Thomas Jefferson to limit Virginia's death penalty to the crimes of murder and treason. The bill was defeated by one vote. In Pennsylvania, Dr. Benjamin Rush, one of the signatories of the Declaration of Independence, argued against the effectiveness of the death penalty as a deterrent. Rush was an early propounder of the theory of the 'brutalization effect', arguing that having the death penalty actually increased criminal behaviour. Pennsylvania was the first state to limit the death penalty, repealing it in 1794 for all offences except first-degree murder.

In the 19th century, many other states limited or repealed the death penalty and constructed state penitentiaries. Other states kept the death penalty, however, and some even expanded the number of capital crimes. In 1888, New York built the first electric chair, using it for the first time to execute one William Kemmler in 1890.

In 1924, the use of cyanide gas was introduced in Nevada as a more 'humane' method of execution. Gee Jon was the first person executed in a gas chamber. The 1930s and 40s saw a sharp rise in executions, in line with criminological thinking holding the death penalty to be a necessary social measure. There were more executions in the 1930s than in any other decade and an average of 167 per year met their deaths.

In the 1950s and 1960s, public opinion again turned away from capital punishment and the number of executions fell sharply, from 1289 in the 1950s

MAIN METHODS USED BY AMERICAN STATES

Method	Jurisdiction
Lethal injection 618 executions since 1976	Alabama, Arizona, Arkansas, California, Colorado, Connecticut, Delaware, Florida, Georgia, Idaho, Illinois, Indiana, Kansas, Kentucky, Louisiana, Maryland, Mississippi, Missouri, Montana, Nevada, New Hampshire, New Jersey, New Mexico, New York, North Carolina, Ohio, Oklahoma, Oregon, Pennsylvania, South Carolina, South Dakota, Tennessee, Texas, Utah, Virginia, Washington, Wyoming, U.S. military, U.S. government
Electrocution 150 executions since 1976	Alabama, Arkansas, Florida, Illinois, Kentucky, Nebraska, Oklahoma, South Carolina, Tennessee, Virginia
Gas chamber 11 executions since 1976	Arizona, California, Maryland, Missouri, Wyoming
Hanging 3 executions since 1976	Delaware, New Hampshire, Washington
Firing squad 2 executions since 1976	Idaho, Oklahoma, Utah

to 715 in the 1960s and only 191 from 1960 to 1976. In 1972, the death penalty was declared unconstitutional and suspended following the Supreme Court's decision in the landmark case Furman v Georgia. The Furman decision stated that the reliance on the jury alone to determine a sentence up to and including the death penalty, could result in arbitrary or capricious treatment, violating the Eighth Amendment prohibition of 'cruel and unusual punishment'. On 29 June 1972, existing death penalty statutes in 40 states were nullified and the death sentences of 629 death row inmates commuted.

States rewrote their statutes in an attempt to eliminate any arbitrariness. Florida's new code appeared only five months after the Furman decision, followed by 34 other states. In 1976 the Supreme Court reinstated the death penalty and the ten-year moratorium came to an end with the execution of Gary Gilmore in 1977.

GEE JON WAS THE FIRST PERSON EXECUTED IN A GAS CHAMBER. THE STATE HAD FIRST TRIED PUMPING CYANIDE INTO JON'S CELL AS HE SLEPT, BUT THIS PROVED UNWORKABLE AND A GAS CHAMBER WAS BUILT.

Death Row

In the United States, prisoners condemned to die are kept apart in a special part of the prison known as Death Row. There they are held, in dismal conditions and often for many years; the average time between sentencing and execution in the US is eight and a half years. Many of those awaiting execution have been there for 10 or even 15 years. As the French writer and philosopher Albert Camus put it: 'The devastating, degrading fear that is imposed on the condemned for months or years is a punishment more terrible than death.'

Black people are sentenced to death and executed in disproportionately greater numbers than whites. Eighty-three per cent of executions since 1976 have involved the murder of a white victim, even though whites are the victims in less than 50 per cent of murders. Examination of the race of both the defendant and the victim reveals an even starker contrast. Since 1976, 117 black defendants have been executed for the murder of a white victim, but only eight white defendants for the murder of a black victim.

Supreme Court Justice Harry Blackmun, himself a supporter of capital punishment, has stated, 'Even under the most sophisticated death penalty statutes, race continues to play a major role in determining who shall live and who shall die.' A recent analysis of capital cases in Philadelphia carefully eliminated factors such as the severity of the crime or the background of the defendant, revealing that black men's chances of receiving a death sentence are nearly four times higher than for white men. Another study found that since the death penalty had been reinstated in Kentucky, there had been over 1000 murders of black people, yet not one of the defendants awaiting execution in Kentucky had killed a black person.

In other parts of the world, the picture is more positive. In August 2002 the Philippines abolished the death penalty and to mark the occasion the Coliseum in Rome was illuminated with golden light for two days. The city government of Rome, in association with Amnesty International, the Vatican and Italian charities, illuminates the Coliseum, the scene of so much death and carnage in ancient times, every time a prisoner is spared execution or a country abolishes the death penalty or announces a moratorium. It was lit in 2000 when Illinois governor George Ryan announced a moratorium on executions in the state.

ABOLITION OF THE DEATH PENALTY SINCE 1976

1976 PORTUGAL abolished the death penalty for all crimes.

1978 DENMARK abolished the death penalty for all crimes.

1979 LUXEMBOURG, NICARAGUA and NORWAY abolished the death penalty for all crimes. BRAZIL, FIJI and PERU abolished the death penalty for ordinary crimes.

1981 FRANCE and CAPE VERDE abolished the death penalty for all crimes.

1982 THE NETHERLANDS abolished the death penalty for all crimes.

1983 CYPRUS and EL SALVADOR abolished the death penalty for ordinary crimes.

1984 ARGENTINA abolished the death penalty for ordinary crimes.

1985 AUSTRALIA abolished the death penalty for all crimes.

1987 HAITI, LIECHTENSTEIN and the GERMAN DEMOCRATIC REPUBLIC abolished the death penalty for all crimes.

1989 CAMBODIA, NEW ZEALAND, ROMANIA and SLOVENIA abolished the death penalty for all crimes.

1990 ANDORRA, CROATIA, the CZECH AND SLOVAK FEDERAL REPUBLIC, HUNGARY, IRELAND, MOZAMBIQUE, NAMIBIA and SAO TOME AND PRINCIPE abolished the death penalty for all crimes.

1992 ANGOLA, PARAGUAY and SWITZERLAND abolished the death penalty for all crimes.

1993 GUINEA-BISSAU, HONG KONG and SEYCHELLES abolished the death penalty for all crimes. GREECE abolished the death penalty for ordinary crimes.

1994 ITALY abolished the death penalty for all crimes.

1995 DJIBOUTI, MAURITIUS, MOLDOVA and SPAIN abolished the death penalty for all crimes.

1996 BELGIUM abolished the death penalty for all crimes.

1997 GEORGIA, NEPAL, POLAND and SOUTH AFRICA abolished the death penalty for all crimes. BOLIVIA and BOSNIA-HERZEGOVINA abolished the death penalty for ordinary crimes.

1998 AZERBAIJAN, BULGARIA, CANADA, ESTONIA and LITHUANIA abolished the death penalty for all crimes.

1999 EAST TIMOR, TURKMENISTAN and UKRAINE abolished the death penalty for all crimes. LATVIA abolished the death penalty for ordinary crimes.

2000 COTE D'IVOIRE and MALTA abolished the death penalty for all crimes. ALBANIA abolished the death penalty for ordinary crimes.

2001 CHILE abolished the death penalty for ordinary crimes.

2002 TURKEY abolished the death penalty for ordinary crimes. THE FEDERAL REPUBLIC OF YUGOSLAVIA and CYPRUS abolished the death penalty for all crimes.

PUNISHMENT TODAY

I t has only been 10,000 years since humans first lived in settled societies – a twinkling of an eye in evolutionary time. We may no longer burn people at the stake or throw them to the lions, but if in the entire history of punishment little appears to have changed, that should not be surprising. Human instincts, actions and motives have not changed much in recorded history and punishment remains, as ever, a combination of retribution, incapacitation and deterrence.

In the 18th century, punishment entered the modern age and Cesare Beccaria called for an end to torture and for punishments that were swift, certain and proportionate. Today, a mere 239 years after *On Crimes and Punishments*, much that Beccaria decried still exists. Official punishments still include the death penalty and corporal punishment, prisons are still run as private businesses, and torture, although universally outlawed, is still regularly practised on every continent.

ALTERNATIVE PUNISHMENTS AND ALTERNATIVES TO PUNISHMENT

Beccaria advocated automatic penalties for each crime, believing that judges should administer the penalties set down in law, rather than interpret the law by setting a sentence. He also believed that a crime should be punished with the minimum penalty necessary to deter. If he were alive today, Beccaria would be happy to see mandatory minimum sentencing in the United States, but would probably be surprised by sentences that are long by 18th-century standards.

Beccaria intended mandatory sentences to protect offenders from capricious decisions, but this approach also prevents the judge from taking into account any mitigating circumstances – from using, in fact, his judgement. A Sharia judge sentencing a criminal to death or amputation would claim to be restricted to prescribing the punishment set down in law. In many American states, judges also have little leeway and are prevented from taking the offender's age, circumstances or lack of any previous criminal record into account.

LEFT: In most countries, imprisonment is the strongest punishment the law allows. The world's prison population is increasing, with calls for longer and longer sentences. Prisons are overcrowded, expensive and of arguable deterrent value, yet no better alternative has emerged.

In December 2002, a British judge took a different approach. A former paedophile, who had previously served time for offences, was charged with a new offence that he had committed years before. He had completed his sentence for the previous charges, undergone counselling and training and had since his release counselled former offenders. Although he pleaded guilty to the charge, the judge decided that no purpose would be served by punishing the offender and that imprisoning him would deprive society of the benefit of his valuable work with ex-offenders.

Even in the harsh punishment regime of the United States, some judges have attempted to use alternatives to custodial sentences, where they exist. These have included electronic surveillance, community service or even drug treatment, education and job training. Schemes in New Mexico, Wisconsin and other states take a pragmatic approach and state that these alternatives are both cheaper than punishment and more effective in preventing crime.

The idea that traditional methods of punishment are not necessarily the best way of fighting crime is not a new one. Chinese philosophy saw punishment as a yin, or negative, influence on behaviour, which was naturally complemented by the yang, or positive, influences such as the family, the village community and trade and religious organizations. Beccaria stated that 'the best ways to prevent crimes are to enact clear and simple laws, reward virtue and improve education.' An effective social network makes fighting crime easier by ensuring that punishment is not the only solution to crime.

RIGHT: Is there ever a justification for the death penalty? This protestor thinks not, demonstrating outside the Federal Penitentiary in Terre Haute, Indiana, where Oklahoma City bomber Timothy McVeigh was due to be executed on June 11, 2001.

In some cases, punishment can either have no impact on crime, or even make the situation worse. American drug policy is one example of this and comparisons are often drawn between the current situation and that experienced during prohibition in the United States when alcohol was illegal from 1920 to 1933. During this period police cells filled with drinkers and barkeepers as violent criminal gangs seized control of the illicit alcohol trade. Intended as a measure against lawlessness, prohibition only contributed to it and over 300,000 convictions did not stop people drinking. A government report of 1931 concluded that prohibition was unenforceable and contributed to lawlessness, and the government eventually decided that the social ills of alcohol were preferable to those of prohibition.

In its attempt to reduce drug use, the American law system makes little distinction between soft and hard drugs, and smugglers, dealers and users alike are punished by mandatory minimum prison sentences. There are over half a million non-violent drug offenders in American prisons – a figure that more than exceeds the total prison population of Western Europe. Europe's relatively soft punitive regimes provide a marked contrast to the system in the United States. Many European countries have decriminalized cannabis in order to refocus police resources on tackling street crime and hard drugs, which are far more dangerous and socially damaging.

Limiting punishment

If you reduce the number of illegal acts, there will be less crime. The idea is not so ridiculous as it sounds. As public opinion changes, laws are repealed – in 19th-century England over 100 capital offences were dropped in a series of legal reforms. As society's values change, certain offences are removed from the list of punishable offences. For instance, homosexuality was initially a crime to be punished, then a disease to be treated, and now is, for the most part but by no means universally, decriminalized and accepted as part of human relationships. The decriminalization of cannabis is another example of social change forcing changes in the law.

Every society limits punishment only to those held to be responsible for their actions. The Tang Code declared an amnesty for the young, the old and the mentally and physically disabled. Equally, in all modern societies there are cases when punishment is deemed inappropriate. An offender may be deemed mentally incapacitated and thereby receives medical treatment instead of punishment. A violent act may be judged to have been an act of self-defence and so is not punished. At the end of a war, instead of retribution against enemy troops, a general amnesty may be declared that absolves ordinary soldiers from guilt. Just such an approach was taken by the Truth and

Reconciliation Commission in South Africa. Thanks largely to the work of the Commission, power passed to the majority black population without significant violence, proving earlier predictions of a bloodbath to be unfounded.

Nelson Mandela's own example was a significant factor in ensuring a peaceful transition. Imprisoned from 1964 to 1990, Mandela was instantly transformed from prisoner to statesman on his release. Mandela appeared free of bitterness or a desire for vengeance against his former oppressors. Elected President in 1994, one of Mandela's first acts was to set up the Truth and Reconciliation Commission, chaired by Bishop Desmond Tutu. The Commission was a unique solution to the problem of how to acknowledge and make reparation for the events of the past, without unleashing the vengeance and bloodshed that has so often marked regime changes in post-colonial Africa.

During its three years in existence the Commission attempted to investigate the entire gruesome legacy of the apartheid years. Police officers, government officials, ANC activists and scores of victims testified before the Commission. Those who confessed their crimes were given amnesty and faced no criminal charges. The Commission applied the same kind of standards as a war trial, which only punishes those responsible for the grossest human rights violations, not soldiers acting under orders.

The Commission had its successes. In 1996, former President F.W. de Klerk appeared before the Commission and begged forgiveness for the years of apartheid. In 1997, Winnie Madikizela-Mandela, the President's ex-wife, was subpoenaed for her part in violent attacks carried out by her bodyguards, the Mandela United Football Club. At its best, the process was a traumatically painful but necessary expiation of the horrors of the past. At other times, truths were half-revealed with officials confessing to some, but not all of their crimes. Only one minister came forward to testify, former Prime Minister P.W. Botha refused to appear and one official after another avoided appearing before the Commission.

The Commission was an extraordinary response to the horrific national disaster of apartheid. In ensuring that the new South Africa did not descend into racial bloodletting it was a success. That it failed to satisfy all of the black population is no surprise. Black South Africans, overwhelmingly the victims of apartheid, had most to lose in the process. Many felt cheated of the right to punish, to see the perpetrators get their just deserts. Justice was exchanged for reconciliation, but as one South African journalist put it: 'How can we be reconciled, if we have never in our history been "conciled"?' The Commission pioneered an entirely new approach to punishment; one that sought above all

'Crime will be with us, and punishment, whether it be draconian or soft, will not eliminate it. But we should seek as best we can, to reduce crime without sacrificing fundamental moral values.' (C.L. Ten, *Crime, Guilt and Punishment*)

LEFT: Robben Island prison, Cape Town Bay, South Africa, February 1994. Four years after his release, President Nelson Mandela returns to the cell he occupied for much of his 27 years' incarceration. Mandela was without bitterness and on election formed the Truth and Reconciliation Commission to investigate apartheid-era abuses and absolve those who came forward and confessed.

else to ensure that justified anger would not be turned into revenge. In Desmond Tutu's words: 'We are looking to maintain not retribution but reparation; we are seeking room for humanity rather than revenge.'

PUNISHMENT: THE VERDICT

What is the verdict on punishment? If the primary aim of punishment is to deter, then it has failed. Punishment can never succeed in eliminating crime and it is debatable whether punishment even has any deterrent effect by itself.

Maximum punishment can deter, as it does in Singapore and Saudi Arabia, but so can minimum punishment, as it does in Denmark. In each of these cases, social factors other than punishment probably do more to keep the crime rates low. That does not mean that punishment makes no difference, just that it cannot cure all the ills of society.

Punishment has never really been given a chance to succeed as it has hardly ever been put into practice as intended. if punishment is applied fairly, if there are no miscarriages of justice, no partiality towards any race or class, no bungling, excess of punishment or torture, and if the penal system is supported by a complementary range of services, then punishment may have a chance of success.

BIBLIOGRAPHY

Baigent, Michael and Richard Leigh. *The Inquisition.* London: Penguin, 2000.

Drapkin, Israel. *Crime and Punishment in the Ancient World.* Lexington, MA: Lexington Press, 1989.

Duff, R. A. and David Garland, eds. *A Reader on Punishment.* Oxford: Oxford University Press, 1994.

Farrington, Karen. *Hamlyn History of Punishment and Torture.* London: Hamlyn, 2000.

Foucault, Michel. *Discipline and Punish* (trans. Alan Sheridan). London: Penguin, 1987.

Garnsey, Peter. *Social Status and Legal Privilege in the Roman Empire.* Oxford: Clarendon, 1970.

Genet, Jean. *The Thief's Journal* (trans. Bernard Frechtman). New York: Grove Press, 1964.

Holt, P. M., Ann K. S. Lambton and Bernard Lewis, eds. *The Cambridge History of Islam* (Volume 2). *Islamic Society and Civilisation.* Cambridge: Cambridge University Press, 1977.

Hucker, Charles O. *China to 1850.* Stanford: Stanford University Press, 1975.

Johnson, Wallace, trans. *The T'ang Code* (volumes 1 & 2). Princeton: Princeton University Press, 1997.

Kerrigan, Michael. *The Instruments of Torture.* Staplehurst, UK: Spellmount, 2001.

Moore, Michael. *Stupid White Men.* London: Penguin, 2002.

Morris, Norval and David J. Rothman, eds. *The Oxford History of the Prison.* Oxford, Oxford University Press, 1998.

Philips, David and Susanne Davies, eds. *A Nation of Rogues? Crime, Law and Punishment in Colonial Australia.* Melbourne: Melbourne University Press, 1994.

WEB LINKS

www.aclu.org: American Civil Liberties Union. A premier US human rights organization.

www.amnesty.org: Amnesty International. News, articles and country-by-country reports on torture and human rights abuses.

www.fsmitha.com/h1/index.html: The Ancient World. Articles on key events in the ancient world, from prehistory to 500 CE.

www.gatewaystobabylon.com/introduction/briefchonology.htm: Brief Chronology of Mesopotamia. Timeline of Mesopotamian civilizations.

www.la.utexas.edu/research/poltheory/beccaria/delitti/index.html: *Cesare Beccaria: On Crimes and Punishments.* English translation of Beccaria's essay.

www.wsu.edu:8080/~dee/MESO/CODE.HTM: The Code of Hammurabi. Complete text of the Code.

www.deathpenaltyinfo.org: Death Penalty Information Center. Meticulously researched articles, reports and statistics on the death penalty worldwide.

www.motherjones.com/prisons: Debt To Society. Special report on the state of US prisons by *Mother Jones* magazine.

www.fordham.edu/halsall/ancient/asbook.html: Internet Ancient History Sourcebook. All the major ancient documents in English translation, most reproduced in full.

www.soas.ac.uk/Centres/IslamicLaw/Materials.html#Articles: Islamic and Middle Eastern Law Materials. Islamic law links compiled by London University's Centre for Islamic and Middle Eastern Law.

www.perseus.tufts.edu: The Perseus Project. Tufts University history site: includes an internal search engine and a library of full-text classical works.

www.roman-empire.net: The Roman Empire. Encyclopaedic detail on all aspects of the Roman Republic and Empire.

www.usccr.gov: United States Commission on Civil Rights. Civil rights reports and findings.

www.corpun.com: World Corporal Punishment Research. A site providing comprehensive information on corporal punishment, with a large press archive.

INDEX

Page numbers in italics
refer to illustrations

Abbasid dynasty 43, 47
Abraham 29
acts of penitence 47
adultery, punishment
  16, 20, 24–5, 27, 35, 45, *49*
Age of Enlightenment, attitudes to
  punishment 105–11, 127–8
alcohol prohibition 45, 49, 50
  effects of 185
Algeria, torture 140
Allah 39, 41
Al-Qaeda suspects 123, *151*
Amnesty International 123, 173, 176–7
  torture 140–1, 142, 143, 151–2
amnesties 185–7
amputation 95–7
  Islamic punishment 45–6, 50
  see also corporal punishment;
    mutilation
Anglo-Saxons, hanging 166
animals, execution by 67, 68, *69*
Anti-terrorism, Crime and Security
  Act (2001, US) 124
apartheid, South Africa 186–7
apostasy see heretics
Arabs *36*, 38, 41, 48
Aristotle *58*
arson, Roman 64, 67
Aryans, India 71–2, *75*
Athens
  death penalty 56–7, 155, 168, 170
  democracy 53–6, 57–8
  homicides 54, 55, 56–7
  legal system 53–5, 56–9
  see also Greece
Augustus 67
auto-da-fé 160–1

Babylon 53
  branding 93
  Code of Hammurabi
    8–9, 21–7, 29–32, 94, 155
banishment *see* exile
bastinado 130, *131*

beatings 141, 146, 148 *see also* flogging
Beccaria, Cesare
  106–7, 128, 153, 183, 184
beheading *see* decapitation
Belmarsh prison, London 124, *125*
Bentham, Jeremy 89, 107–11
Bible 14, 155
  Biblical laws 8, 29–35, 37–8
black people, executing *178*, 180
Blackmun, Justice Harry 180
blood feuds, prehistoric societies 11, 12
blood money
  Athenian 54, 55
  Islamic law 44, 46–7, 50
Bluebeard (Henri Desiré Landru) 171–2
boot camps *102*
brahmans, India 72, 73, 74, 75
brainwashing 147–8, *149*, *150*
branding *97*, 141
  British 93, *94*, *95*
  Roman 68, 93
  see also corporal punishment
Brazil, prisons 123
Bridewell workhouse, London 112
Britain
  amputation punishment 95–7
  branding 93, *94*, *95*
  flogging 85–6, *87*
  pillory and stocks 98, *100*
  torture 138
  see also England
brutalization effect 178
burning
  at the stake 64, 67, 156, 168
  execution by 35, 157–62
  torture 142, 151
  trial by ordeal *132*, 133
Byzantine empire 66

cangue pillory *70*, 98
capital punishment *see* death penalty
caste system, India 71–2, 73, 74, 75
cat o'nine tails *84*, 85
Central Criminal Court, London
  113, 115
chain gangs *122*
Chile, torture 141

China
  death penalty 79, 80–1, 82, *83*,
    173, 174, 177
  early history 76–7
  legal systems 8, 71, 77–83, 185
  philosophy of punishment 184
  pillories *70*, 98
  political prisoners 141
  punishments *70*, 77, 78, 79
  torture *76*, 81, 82, 127, 130, 140–1
Christians, burning to death 157
Cicero 63
Claudius 68
Code of Hammurabi 8–9, 21–7, 29–32,
  94, 155
Code of Justinian 66
collective prosecution, China 80–1
community service 184
Confucius 78, *79*
Constantine 66, 68
contract law, Babylonian 27
corporal punishment
  Chinese 77, 79, 81, 83
  Indian 74, 76
  Roman 64, 68
  see also amputation; flogging;
    mutilation
Council of Aeropagus *54*, 55
court records 16–17, 24
courts
  Central Criminal Court, London
    113, 115
  Indian 74–5, 76
  judicial torture 68, 127, *128*, 133
  Roman 65–6, 67
Coustos, John 134–6
crucifixion *65*, 67–8, 162

death of a thousand cuts 130–1
death penalty
  abolition *175*, 176, 178, 181
  Athenian 56–7, 168, 170
  Babylonian 27
  Biblical law 32, 35, 37–8
  black people *178*, 180
  Chinese 79, 80–1, 82, *83*, 173, 174, 177
  Code of Hammurabi 25, 26, 27, 155

English 157, 170
Indian 74
Islamic 45–6
Laws of Eshunna 19–20
opposition to 106–7, 175–6, *177*,
    179–80, *184*
Roman 60, *62*, 63–4, 67–8
Sumerian 17
US 117, *176*, 177–80
see also execution methods
Death Row 180
deaths, prison 111, 115
debtors slavery 57, 58–9, 64
decapitation 35, 37, *156*, 157
    see also guillotine
China 79, 80–1, 82, *83*, 173, 174, 177
democracy, Athenian 53–6, 57–8
Denmark, prisons 124–5
deterrence 105–7, 108, 173
Dickens, Charles 119, 121
Discipline and Punish 103–4
discretionary punishments, Islamic
    law *42*, 45
disease, prison 111, 115, 116
disorientation, prisoners 149, 151
divorce, Babylonian 24–5
dowry, Babylonian 24–5
Draco, Athenian law 9, 56–7
drowning, death penalty 25, 27
drugs
    offenders 121, 123, 177, 185
    torture 152–3
Duke's Laws, New York 178

egalitarianism *see* equality
Egypt, control by Hebrews 29–30
electric chairs *154*, 172–3, 179
electric shock torture 143–6
electronic surveillance 184
England
    death penalty 7, 157, 166–8, 170–1
    legal system 108, *113*, 115
    religious persecution 161
    witch-hunting 140, 142, 162
    see also Britain
Enlightenment, attitudes to
    punishment 105–11, 127–8
equality 12, 18, 30
    Babylonian society 21, 23
    Islamic law 38, 39
Eshunna 18–20
European colonialism,

effect on Arab nations 48
execution methods *62*, *69*, 170
    burning 35, 64, 67, 156, 157–62, 168
    crucifixion *65*, 67–8, 162
    decapitation 35, 37, 79, *80*, *83*,
        156, 157
    electric chair *154*, 172–3, 179
    French 103–4, 163–6
    gas chamber death penalty 179, 180
    hanging 67, 68, 117, 157, 166–8,
        178, *179*
    lethal injection 172, 173, *179*
    poison 168, 170
    shooting 173–5, *179*
    stoning *33*, *34*, 35, 37, *44*, 45, *49*, 50
    see also death penalty
executioners
    Albert Pierrepoint 173
    Charles-Henri Sanson *164*, 165
    Thomas Marwood 167–8
exile
    Athenian 56–7, 170
    Biblical law 32–3
    Chinese 78, 79, 81
    Indian 74
    Roman 67, 68–9

Fawkes, Guy *167*, 168
Fay, Michael 91–2
fear, torture provoking 129–30, 137,
    145–6
fines 16–18, 73, 82, 117
    Babylonian 23–4
    Biblical law 34, 35
    Roman 7, 63, 69
firing squads *see* shooting
Fleet Prison, London 114
flogging 45, 50, 85–90
    Biblical law 34–5
    Roman 64, 68
    today 90–3
    US 117, 120
    workhouses 112
    see also beatings
Foucault, Michel 103–4
France 103–4
    guillotine 163, *164*, 165, 171–2
Fry, Elizabeth *113*, *114*
furca, Roman executions 67, 68

gallows *see* hanging
gaol fever 115, 116

gas chambers 179, 180
Gilgamesh, King of Uruk *10*, 13, *15*
Gilmore, Gary *172*, 174–5, 180
Great Wall, China 77
Greece, ancient 7, *158 see also* Athens
Guantanamo Bay, Cuba 123, *151*
Guatemala, death by shooting *174*
guillotine 163–6, 171–2
    see also decapitation

hadd Islamic punishments 44–6, 51
hadith traditions 41, 43, 44
Halifax gibbet 163, 165, 168
Hammurabi king of Babylon 18
    Code 8–9, 21–7, 29–32, 94, 155
hanging 27, 117, 157, 162, 166–8,
    178, *179*
    Roman 67, 68
hanging, drawing and quartering
    9, 103–4, 168
Hearst, Patty 147, *150*
Hebrews *20*, 29–30
heretics 46, 86–7
    burning to death 156, 159, 160–1
    see also Spanish Inquisition
Hesiod 53–4, 55, 56, 57
highwaymen
    Chinese *70*
    Islamic 45–6
Hinduism, India 71–2
Holland, prisons *105*, 115
Homer 54, 55
homicide 32, 60, 81
    Athenian law 54, 55, 56–7
Hopkins, Matthew,
    'Witchfinder-General' 140, 142, *162*
Howard, John 114–16
humiliation, of prisoners 151–2
hunger strikes, Turkish 123

Iliad 54, 55
incest 12, 35
India
    caste system 71–2, 73, 74, 75
    death penalty 74
    legal systems 8, 71, 72–6, 94
    punishments 73, 74
    torture 138, 142
Inquisition of Rome *159*
Inquisition, Spanish
    see Spanish Inquisition
Iran 92

Iraq 13, 21
Iron Maiden 131, 133
Islam 38–40
   after Mohammed 47–8
   Sharia law 8, 29, *40*, 41–47, *49*,
      50–1, 95, 97
   20th century 48–51, 92
Israel, torture 142

Jackson, Jesse 122
Jewish law *see* Biblical laws
Judge Dee (Di Renjie) 82
judges 26–7, 55, 100–1, 183–4
judicial torture 68, 127, *128*, 133
   see also Spanish Inquisition
juries
   Roman 66, 67
   US 117, 180
Justinian, Code of 66

King, Martin Luther, Jr. *123*
King, Rodney 146
kings
   Babylonian 21–3, 25
   Louis XVI *163*, 165–6
   Mesopotamian *10*, 15–16
kittee 138
Koran 39, 41, 43, 44, 50 *see also* Islam

Landru, Henri Desiré (Bluebeard)
   171–2
lashings *see* flogging
law of precedent,
   Code of Hammurabi 22–7
Laws of Eshunna 18–20
Laws of Manu, India 71, 73–6, 94
legal systems
   Athenian 53–5, 56–9
   Biblical 8, 29–35, 37–8, 155
   Chinese 71, 77–83
   Code of Hammurabi 21–7
   English 108, *113*, 115
   Eshunnan 18–20
   Indian 71, 72–6, 94
   Roman 53, 60, 61–7
   Sharia law 8, 29, *40*, 41–7, *49*, 50–1, 92
   Urgakina 15–16
   Ur-Nammu 15, 16–18
legislation, public opinion affecting 185
lethal injections 172, 173, *179*
Louis XVI, death by guillotine
   163, 165–6

McVeigh, Timothy *184*
magistrates *see* judges
Malaysia, political prisoners 123
Malleus Maleficarum 161
Manava Dharmasastra 71, 73–6, 94
Manchurian Candidate, The 147, *149*
Mandela, Nelson 186, *187*
Manu *see* Laws of Manu
Marwood, Thomas 167–8
Mayan civilisation *129*
Mecca 38, 40
mental torture 146–53
Mesopotamia *10*, 13–20, 29
Middle Ages, death by burning
   156, 157, 159
Mohammed *36*, 38–40, 41, 45
Moses 30
murder *see* homicide
mutilation 94–7 *see also* amputation;
   corporal punishment
Mycaenean civilisation 53

naming and shaming 99–101
Nero 65, 67, 68, 157
Newgate prison, London 112–13, *114*,
   167, 170–1
Nigeria, Sharia law *40*, *49*, 50–1, 97

Odyssey 54
Old Bailey *see* Central Criminal Court
On Crimes and Punishments 106–7,
   128, 183, 184
OPEC (Organization of Petroleum
   Exporting Countries) 49–50
open prisons 124–5
ordeal, trial by 75, *132*, 133
Ottoman Empire 48, 49
overcrowding, prisons 111, 112–13

paedophiles 184
patricians, Roman 60–1
penitence 47
   heretics 86–7
Penitentiary Act (1779) 115–16
penitentiary system, US
   111, 119–20, 179
Pentonville prison, London 111
Persia *see* Iraq
piercing, torture by 133, 142
Pierrepoint, Albert 173
pillory 96, 98, *100*, 101
plebeians, Roman 60–1

poison 168, 170
police forces
   Indian 75
   Roman 65, 67
political prisoners 123, 141
politics, Arab regional 49–50
prehistoric societies 7, 11–12
'pressed to plead' *135*, 136–7
prison reform *114*, 115–16, 117, *118*,
   119–20
prisoners *20*, *28*, *102*, *105*, *118*, *122*, *182*
   drug offenders 185
   floggings *84*, 88–9
   labour 112, 116, 119, *122*
   of war 142, 147, *149*
prisons
   Age of Enlightenment *109*, 110–17
   alternatives to 184
   Belmarsh, London 124, *125*
   boot camps *102*
   chain gangs *122*
   conditions 111–17, 119–20, 123–5
   costs 121–3
   Danish 124–5
   death rates 111, 115
   diseases 111, 115, 116
   Dutch *105*, 115
   effectiveness 120–1, 184–5
   French 104
   Guantanamo Bay, Cuba 123, *151*
   Newgate 112–13, *114*, 167, 170–1
   open 124–5
   Panopticon *109*, 110–11
   re-education camps 148–9
   solitary confinement 110, 116, 123
   Tower of London 111–12, 137
   US *102*, *110*, 111, 117–23, *184*
prosecution, collective 80–1
public executions 170–2
   see also death penalty
public opinion, effect on laws 185

Quakers 87, 93, 95
quartering 9, 103–4, 168

rack *52*, *128*, 133–6, 137, *158*
Raleigh, Sir Walter 156
rape 112, 141
   Babylonian law 26, 27
Rationale of Punishment, The 89
reconciliation 186–7
re-education camps 148–9

rehabilitation 106, 119–20
retaliation *see* talio
Roman Catholics
  executions *167*, 168
  persecution by *159*, 160–1
Rome, ancient 60
  branding 93
  death penalty 60, *62*, 63–4, 67–8,
    155, 157, 163
  legal systems 53, 60, 61–7
  punishments 7, 52, 63–4, *65*, 67–9,
    85, 93
Rush, Benjamin 178

Sanson, Charles-Henri *164*, 165
Saudi Arabia 92, 97
Scavenger's Daughter *136*, 137
scourging *see* flogging
sentences
  mandatory 106–7, 121, 185
  role of judges 100–1, 183–4
sex crimes 44–5, 100–1
shaming 99–101
Sharia law 8, 29, *40*, 41–47, 92
  amputation 95, 97
  re-emergence *49*, 50–1
shooting, execution by 173–5, *179*
Sing Sing prison, New York 119, *120*
Singapore 7, 90–2
slavery
  Chinese 81
  debtors 57, 58–9, 64
slaves
  Babylonian 18, 23–4, 26
  punishments 67–8, 88–9, *97*, 127
sleep deprivation 140
Socrates, death penalty 168, 170
solitary confinement 110, 116, 123
Solon, Athenian law 57–9
Soviet Union, torture *140*, 152–3
Spanish Inquisition 86–7, *169*
  auto-da-fé 160–1

torture *126*, 130, 131, 134–6,
  138–9, 158
State of the Prisons in England, The 115
statistics
  executions 157, 176–7, 179–80
  prisons 121, 123, 185
stocks 64, 96, 98, *99*, 101
stoning 16, 67
  Biblical law *33*, *34*, 35, 37
  Islamic law *44*, 45, *49*, 50
stun weapons 143–6
Sumerians 13–20, 22–7
sunna 41, 42–3, 50

talio 11, 21
  Code of Hammurabi 21, 23, 25, 27
  Islamic punishment 44, 46–7, 50
Tang Code, China 8, 71, 77–83, 185
tasers 146
tattooing 93
Ten Abominations, China 79–80, 81
Ten Commandments 30–1
Texas, shaming punishments 99–101
thumbscrews *137*, 138
torture
  abolition 128
  Chinese *76*, 81, 82, 127, 130, 140–1
  judicial 68, 127, 133
  methods *126*, 130–53
  opposition to 106–7, 127–8
  Roman *52*, 68
  Soviet Union *140*, 152–3
  Turkish 123, 130, 151, *153*
  United Nations Convention 130, 141
  US *139*, 144–5, 146
Tower of London 111–12, 137
treadmills *84*
trials
  Athenian 54–5
  by juries 66, 67, 117, 180
  by ordeal 75, 132, 133
  Indian 74–5

Roman 64, 68
Truth and Reconciliation Commission
  185–7
Turkey 11, 48
  political prisoners 123
  torture 120, 130, 151, *153*
Twelve Tables, Roman laws 60, 61–5
Tyburn, London 170–1

United Nations Convention on torture
  130, 141
United States
  death penalty 117, 176, 177–80
  Death Row 180
  execution methods 172–3
  floggings 117, 120
  prison reform 117, *118*, 119–20
  prisons *102*, *110*, 111, 117–23, *184*
  torture *139*, 144–5, 146
  treatment of slaves 88–9, *97*
Universal Declaration of Human
  Rights 176
Ur dynasties 15–18
Urgakina legal code 15–16
Ur-Nammu legal code 15, 16–18
Uruk, Sumeria 13–14

Vietnam, re-education camps 148–9

Wahhabism 48–9
water torture *126*, 138–40
wheel, execution on 170
whipping *see* flogging
witches 35, 140, 142
  burning of 156, 159, 161–2
women
  Babylonian society 24–7
  burning of 168
  floggings 87, 88–9, 93
  Islamic law *42*, 49, 50, 93
  Spanish Inquisition *169*
workhouses 112

PICTURE CREDITS

AKG London: 22, 25, 76, 126, 128, 158, 167, 169, 178
Amber Books: 97
Amnesty International: 143, 145
Corbis: 6, 88, 91, 104, 118, 120, 125
Heritage Image Partnership: 72
Hulton/Getty: 135

Mary Evans Picture Library: 10, 13, 15, 17, 19, 20, 31, 32, 33, 34, 36, 39, 42, 52, 54, 58, 59, 61, 62, 65, 66, 75, 79, 84, 86, 90, 94, 95, 96, 100, 105, 106, 113, 131, 132, 136, 139, 140, 156, 162, 163, 164
Patrick Mulrey: 175, 176
The Picture Desk, Kobal Collection: 149

POPPERFOTO: 28, 40, 44, 46, 49, 70, 80, 92, 99, 101, 107, 114, 116, 134, 150, 151, 153, 154, 172, 174, 177, 179, 184, 187
Topham Picturepoint: 9, 12, 69, 83, 102, 109, 110, 122, 123, 124, 129, 137, 147, 159, 160, 166, 171, 182